'Til Death

A Story of Survival and Renewal

Suzanne C. Sachnowitz Syme, D. Min.

FIRST EDITION
Copyright©20004
By Suzanne C. Sachnowitz
www.goodgrieving.com
ALL RIGHTS RESERVED.
1 2 3 4 5 6 7 8 9
1-57168-855-2
Library of Congress Control Number: 2004110081

Cover design by
Maurice Henderson
West Cork, Ireland

'Til Death

A Story of Survival and Renewal

"Lift the veil and see yourself as your own person–some who will have friends and family and experiences very different from before, but also someone who is capable of doing what needs to be done and doing it with a certain pride and satisfaction. That is the enabling moment.

"My husband believed that life was to be lived–a banquet to be savored. He would want me to continue living. On our very last journey home from Ireland he mentioned to me, 'Suzanne, if anything happens to me, I want you to consider building a life for yourself in Ireland. You could do that.'

"He was right. It is not easy, but life is a gift so precious that to squander it by wallowing in self-pity of anger is to waste it."

–Suzanne Sachnowitz Syme

Acknowledgments

A heartfelt thanks to Eakin Press for their daring to take a chance on a first-time author.

To Chuck Myers, whose literary editorship gave me his wisdom as well as his craft.

To Sheila Coates, who transcribed multiple tapes and who listened not only with her ears, but with her heart, as well.

And most of all to Mickey Herskowitz, whose unfailing encouragement and tenacity made this book possible.

Contents

A Mist Through My Hands

CHAPTER 1

$\mathcal{T}$he day my husband died was a cruelly beautiful day. It was one of those rare days in early spring when the sky is azure blue, the sun warm and golden, the earth green and bursting with renewal. It was a glorious day to be alive, but at 5:30 p.m. our family was meeting at the hospital to disconnect my husband from his life support system.

It was not a good day to die. The earth should have wept and heaved with grief as we did.

Three weeks earlier, my husband, Larry Sachnowitz, who had helped build and then owned a popular Houston advertising agency, had a four-way heart by-pass. It was slick, in and out in 45 minutes. Then, it was time to take him off the heart lung machine, the pump. He did not respond. I knew we were in trouble when all my inquiries about his progress in surgery were vaguely put off. When the surgeon's head nurse came out to the waiting room and told us the doctor would like to see us in the private family room, I knew real fear. Fear was to become my constant companion for a very long time.

The first crisis was whether or not my husband could be weaned off his pump before eight hours, after which his blood would be destroyed. If he stayed on the pump, he would never leave the operating room. This was a routine surgery on a man who had heart disease but no stroke or heart attack yet. He should have been sitting up, complaining about his Jell-O, but instead he was waging the first of several fights for his life. How could this happen? What went wrong? There was very little time to speculate on these questions because heroic medical measures were being initiated.

After a few hours, his heart began to respond, at least on the left side. He was now put on a heart machine that would help keep him alive in the hope that his own heart had perhaps been shocked and would recover its own function.

Our family breathed a sigh of relief. He would be alive in the morning, and, while there was life, we still clung to hope. This artificial heart machine created its own problems, however. It didn't generate a pressure as your own heart would, so major edema resulted. Now we had added pulmonary and renal failure to our problems. Ultimately, he had about 20 liters of fluid extracted. Finally, the decision was made with the heart transplant team to place him on a thoracic pump, which worked much better for him. Despite six returns to surgery and multiple complications, he seemed to be stabilizing, and the prospect of him being a heart transplant candidate was looking up.

Every day, several times a day, we would be at the bedside. All of our children were in town, keeping vigil. I got very savvy at reading the numbers on the various monitors – oxygen rates, blood pressure, liver enzyme. A change in any of these made me encouraged or discouraged. It was an emotional roller coaster. Then the time came to wake him up. He did not respond. Maybe in a couple of days; after all he has had massive doses of anesthesia, paralyzing drugs and sedatives. Still, there was very little, if any, activity from Larry during that period that you could attribute to a willing consciousness on his part.

Now I was feeling desperate. My husband was slipping deeper and deeper into a coma, like mist through my hands. I prayed, Oh, how I prayed for him to open his eyes and look at me. I harangued God to let him recover. I pleaded a case that I had never asked for small stuff, and I had paid, prayed and obeyed all my life. I wanted God to ante up now. Where were you, God, when I needed you?

I was for a long time very angry with God for allowing such a good man as my husband, to die far too soon while evil people lived and died of old age in their beds. At night I would fall into bed exhausted, but sleep was very fitful. I needed sleep badly and was grateful for the few hours of forgetting it offered. But each time I awoke, there was that awful moment when what was happening came back to me, and it was like a physical blow to my stomach. I doubled over in pain at the thought of what was occurring, and worse, what might happen. It became almost impossible to eat; the mere sight or smell of food made me nauseous.

Like a robot, I got up, dressed, drove to the hospital and watched and waited as teams of skilled physicians and nurses did everything possible to restore my husband to health. Even if he survived, there would have been impairment. His fingers and toes developed gangrene, his left leg had been operated on to relieve the pressure, and he might have a drop foot. Could he speak, could he think, would his mind ever recover? Now a new terror arose.

What if he physically recovered but was so neurologically damaged he wasn't really there? Above all else, he would hate this.

Heartbeats:
- Fear is a great motivator but it extracts its own price.
- God may hear our prayers but sometimes the answer is no.
- There is no "routine surgery," each of us is a complex of so many unknowns that can affect the outcome.
- In every major surgery there is a risk of failure, someone will fall into that category of that small percentage. When it's your loved one it is 100 percent.

The Sixth Day

CHAPTER 2

*S*ix days before he died, I knew he wasn't going to make it. This happened to be on the anniversary of the day we met. That night, I truly lost it. I remember being in bed and sobbing hysterically. It's almost a primal moan that erupts when the reality of what is occurring finally hits.

My children were taking turns staying at the house, and I woke my daughter and her husband. Their bedroom was a full floor above me. Amy came downstairs and stayed with me. I remember sobbing like a little kid who can't catch a breath until finally I fell asleep. Now it had become, for me, a death vigil.

The head of our medical team recommended giving the family a few more days to come to grips with this and to be certain beyond a doubt that the situation was hopeless. Then we would set a time to disconnect. Six days and counting, five days, and so on. By now I am not fit to drive, so one of the children has to bring me back and forth from the hospital.

Complicating this is the fact that my husband had a business that depended on his creative talent. How much to tell even the employees is very difficult. We wanted everyone to carry on in the hope that he would return and be his old self. Clients needed to feel that all was well, that he would soon be back with his brilliant marketing strategies and his dynamite creative ideas. We could ill-afford to have staff or clients bolt. During this time, the stock market took a nosedive. We were, unfortunately, heavily margined, so now margin calls were coming in. Here I have a husband who is incompetent and never gave power of attorney to anyone.

I have since become a fanatic on the subject of seeing that affairs are in order, no matter what your age. Otherwise, this can only create incredible obstacles and grief for a spouse. Had my husband lived much longer, I would have had to go before a judge with a doctor's verification and a lawyer's document stating my husband was incompetent so I could be appointed his guardian. My brilliant, charming, creative husband incompetent? He was born competent. This can't be happening.

Meanwhile, back at the hospital, our friends were literally keeping us going. They sent in meals for us for weeks, took care of my dog, shopped, ran errands, offered to baby-sit the grandchildren and gave us the moral support so dearly needed and appreciated. Our rabbis were wonderful; they prayed with us and for us, wept with us and kept vigil when that was really all anyone could do.

Lest you think I inhabit the land of sainthood, think again. Some people were just plain nosy. Others offered comfort in such unctuous tones you could strangle them. We had lived a wonderful life and should still be doing so. All people don't rejoice at your good fortune. Some were a little pleased to see that someone who had it all, and in my mind we did, was getting brought down to earth. We had a really good, not perfect, but a solid marriage. We had a successful business that allowed us to pursue a full and rewarding lifestyle. We shared many interests, including our dream of a home in Ireland. We loved that home and the place and people. We were going to retire there for at least half the year. Actually, the last week of my husband's life, before the hospital, was spent there, which was his happiest. We have eight children, 10 grandchildren, and, at this time, four on the way; we traveled, we entertained, we pursued our musical and intellectual interest. We really did have it all. I had much to lose.

There are those who derive a certain superiority when something like this happens to someone like me. As long as I didn't buy into anybody else's craziness, I could cope. The Irish have a saying – they forget nothing and forgive less. There were moments when I felt like that.

Heartbeats:

• Expect a meltdown when your worst fears are realized.

• No matter what your age or circumstances, have your affairs in order.

• Depend on your friends and loved ones, let them do for you, you'll have plenty of time to be on your own.

• Trust your instincts, they're probably right, but at least they're yours and no one knows you like yourself.

Saying Goodbye

CHAPTER 3

*N*ow the day has come, the dreaded day when we need to go to the hospital to disconnect my husband from his support system. I knew I needed to create some memory of this horrible day that would be a happy memory, so I chose to take my then youngest grandson for a walk in the stroller since the weather was magnificent.

My neighbor across the street has a large tree with an old-fashioned porch swing. I sat there with Ethan, my daughter Kathy's baby. We swung, he slept, and I just drank in the peace of this precious child, his breathing, the beautiful air and the warmth of the sun. I knew I had to imprint in my mind some lovely memory that would be part of an otherwise horrific day.

When we arrived at the hospital, there was a special room set aside for the family as had been explained to us earlier. (I need to make mention of how amazing this experience was for all of us. Actually, everyone deserves to die with the attention and dignity that my husband did and with the care and the comfort that our family received.)

They were waiting for us: the physician who was head of his team, two other physicians, two rabbis and a medical ethicist. There are in my family 15 adults, so this was a fairly good-sized group. At the time Dr. Reardon explained to us what Larry's condition was, he offered us the opportunity to ask questions of him, of the neurologist, of anyone who was involved in his case who could answer questions we might have yet unanswered. Once that was done, he said he would begin to take us back one at a time to say whatever we needed to say to Larry. He offered to spend the entire night there with us. He said to take as long as it took, which was a wonderful gift.

Before we went back, however, I wanted to take that moment to tell our kids how amazingly proud I was of them, and how wonderful they had been in terms of being supportive. It was very difficult for them. They have businesses, careers, small kids; these are young families with a lot of pressures of their own. I told them that death was a very powerful force, but that stronger than death was the love of this family. In the days that followed that proved to be the truth.

The first person to go back, of course, was me. Each of us was accompanied by a doctor on one arm and a rabbi on the other so that, should we feel faint, we'd have someone to hold us up. That contact, the touching, was so important. Knowing there was another human being or two near to care for you and support you was a wonderful, wonderful reassurance.

I went back with the doctor and the rabbi and spent time with my husband. The nursing staff had removed him from the general ICU to a small private section. They had shaved him, had shampooed his hair, he looked clean, he smelled good. I was very grateful for this because these were going to be our last memories of him. He was very, very sick and had very little brain function at the time, which was obviously why we had made the decision, or the medical team had made the decision, that the time had come to disconnect.

I gave him the Irish blessing:

"May the road rise up to meet you. May the wind be always at your back, May the sun shine warm upon your face, May the rain fall soft upon your fields and until we meet again, May God hold you in the palm of his hand."

I kissed him and told him farewell; that it was okay to go home now, he didn't need to fight anymore. I went back and gave the children an opportunity to see him privately. The kids went in one at a time, two at a time for those who were married, and spent as much time as they chose with him. When we all had a chance to do this, and were back in the room again, the doctor asked us if we were ready to do the disconnecting?

We said, yes, we were. Each of us had our moment to say what we wanted to say. Those who chose to be with him at his bedside did so, Kevin, who chose to sit outside, did so. The machine was disconnected, he was given a lot of morphine in the event he could possibly feel any pain. Certainly no one wanted him to suffer.

The expectation was that this would take maybe five to 10 minutes. My husband, in his own irascible style, managed to stay off this machine and alive, reversing a thoracic heart pump, which I think created medical history, for almost two hours.

Anyone who knew Larry, knew he was never on time. He had a great sense of rhythm, a great sense of style, but no sense of time. He took his own sweet time to finally allow his body to just be at peace. He so wanted to be alive. He was such a vital human being that even when he was barely, barely functioning he was fighting to stay alive. We always joked with him that he would be late for his own funeral, and it was appearing as though this could be a prophecy soon fulfilled.

The nursing staff brought us coffee and juice because this was getting to be a pretty long vigil. The doctor put a chair next to my husband's bed, and I sat there and put my head on his heart. I just held him and listened to his heart beating slower and slower. Of course, my skill at monitor reading was such by now that I was able to see that he was diminishing. When his heart had finally beat its last beat, I closed his eyes, we covered him and we left him. A couple of the boys...my one son-in-law and a couple of the sons wished to spend a little more time with him, which they did. It was about 10:30 in the evening. We had been in this process for five hours.

We went back to my house, including my brothers who were in from New York and New Jersey, who had been staying with us, opened a bottle of champagne, and toasted Larry's life because, if ever there was a human being who lived every moment to the fullest, it was my husband.

Suddenly, the realization that he was gone – gone from me, gone from the world, gone from life itself, was incomprehensible. Nature gives us many wonderful gifts, which is why I use the word gifts so frequently. Despite the worst wound I had ever felt, had ever experienced in my life, I know I have been gifted in many, many ways by many, many people.

Nature is kind to you, too. The mind wraps itself around only that which it can handle, so my memory was becoming very dysfunctional. I would look at people I had known forever and go totally blank. I could not remember the name, I could not remember the circumstances. My doctor said to me, "You need to come see me." When I went to see her she said, "What's going on with you physically?" I told her I was not sleeping very well, I was hardly eating at all, and now I was having these memory lapses. She said it was a perfectly normal thing, it was the way the mind was enabling me to cope with this trauma.

As an aside, many people automatically suggest, not physicians by the way, that because there was so much stress connected with my husband's death, I should be "taking something." I should be taking a sedative, I should be taking a sleeping pill, I should be taking something. I know people for whom that is not only helpful, it is critical. But, I am not one of those people, and I strongly suggest that before anybody automatically jumps into taking medication, they make sure it's something they need.

Grief is a debt that has to be paid, and pain accompanies that debt, horrific pain that you pay now or you pay later. When you pay later, the price is ratcheted up significantly, and it may come out in totally inappropriate ways. Now, I was learning about this kind of pain and, damn it, I was determined to own it; I was going to deal with it, and I was going to come out the other end stronger. For myself, for my family and, perhaps even most of all, for my husband, who would have wanted this. Above all else, he would never want me to throw in the towel and give up on life. Soon, I sought the advice of a woman who offers grief counseling, a woman I have known for a long time and in whom I have great confidence. That is a piece of advice I would share with everyone. Talk to somebody, find somebody who's sensitive to what you're experiencing and who can help walk you through it.

Ultimately, you do walk yourself through it. One step at a time, one day at a time, you get up in the morning and face another day. And everyday is awful because everyday you wake up and there's that fraction of a second when you look to the right of you or the left of you wherever your partner slept, and there's nobody there. You think, "Oh, he got up earlier…Oh, he took the dog for a walk…Oh, he's working at the computer." Then you realize, no, he's gone, he's really, really gone. He's not on a business trip, he's gone, he will never ever come back.

The definition of death is never. Everything else in my life I had been able to negotiate, or survive, or work around. You may have to pay a heavy price, the terms may be dear, but it's doable. There is no negotiating with death. Death's debt is not one that is up for grabs.

Death is forever and death is irrevocable. Since both my parents are in their mid-80's and living in their family home and driving and independent and self sufficient, for which we thank God, I had never really had to deal with a significant loss. I had not had anyone very close to me die, so I was and still am on a learning curve here.

To lose your spouse is to lose your heart. In many ways, my heart and my soul had gone with him, so there was a terrible hole and a terrible wound, a terrible emptiness and nothing but lots and lots of time, I presume, will help me begin to heal. You have to heal. I think it must be something like a major surgery through lots of muscle. You heal from the inside out. I'm assuming that I'm healing gradually, little by little, from the inside out.

After we had made the decision to disconnect, and after we had returned to the house, we now had to face the realities and the practicalities of a funeral. I knew this would be a very big funeral because my husband had so many friends, so many associates, and so many contacts, so many people who would be there. We felt there would be a great outpouring, and there was. We guesstimate somewhere between 1,100 and 1,500 people came to his funeral. He had a wonderful send off, he would have loved it. He had a flair for the dramatic and he would have reveled in his exit. He was eulogized by two rabbis and by his son Lanny, who was magnificent, truly magnificent.

Larry would have been thrilled. The funeral director had a 1957 classic Cadillac hearse, which we ordered because Larry owned a 1957 car when he was a kid. I thought this would be something he would like -- to go in style. As the Irish say, "He had a great send-off." During the midst of this, I was borne up by my eldest sons, Jay and David. I had given birth to these two splendid men, now they were literally holding me up and as I looked around my grandson, James, was supporting his mother.

One has to realize that even in the midst of all this, there are moments that are funny, there is humor. When it came time for us to pick out the casket and the container, we had a wonderful funeral director come to the house. We did not have to go to the funeral parlor itself. And since this was a Jewish funeral, there were certain restrictions – we had to have a certain kind of a casket, a certain kind of a container, a certain preparation of the body, certain garments for the burial. We did have to work around some of this, however, mostly because Larry was, amongst other things, a real clothes horse.

I knew being buried in a white shroud would not have been my husband's idea of a great way to go. I spoke to the rabbi about this, and he said, "If the body is prepared properly, and if the body is in the white shroud, we could, yes, put the Armani suit over it, which we did. So Larry's son and I went upstairs to pick out the suit and the shoes and the socks, and I foolishly asked the funeral director, "Do we provide underwear?" He looked at me and said, "Did he wear underwear?" I said, "on a regular basis." He said, "I suggest you send underwear", so underwear went.

We sat around the dining room table looking at all the caskets. We also were writing the obit right there at the table at the same time. This allowed us, through the miracle of modern technology, to send the notice immediately to the newspaper, and we could edit it on site. It was perfect.

I looked at all of these caskets and I said to the director, "What is the most expensive casket you have?"

He said, "pardon me?"

I said, "What is the most expensive casket you have?"

He showed it to me, and I said, "That's the one we want."

He was stunned.

I said, "No really, that's the one we want."

He said, "I have never, ever had anybody do that before."

I said, "Well, if this were my funeral, I would have wanted the plainest, simplest box you have. I would have wanted you to put me in a white shroud and bury me thus because I have no great love for putting money in the ground. However, this is not my funeral, this is Larry's funeral, and he always said, 'I want the most expensive casket.' So, since it was his money, and since it was his funeral, we're doing the most expensive casket."

That offered us a little moment of levity in an otherwise pretty grim experience.

In the Jewish tradition, we sit Shivah, which means we had people coming for seven nights for a short service at home, a meal and for an opportunity for people to come be with us and each other and remember Larry. We would tell jokes about Larry and recount his life. In our tradition it is life that counts, and life that goes forward. It was very healing to actually have people there and to know they would be there every night, that I would not be alone.

By the end of Shivah, however, I was beginning to feel the need to be alone. I needed some downtime. That is probably psychologically why it's designed and structured the way it is. Adding to the complications for me, this was the last night of Shivah, and I was deathly ill. A very dear friend, a nurse, took me upstairs and said, "You're going to bed." I was really, really sick, so my son had to stay with me. I thought, *It's the stress, or it's the flu, or it's the whatever.* But, days went on, and I just didn't seem to get any better.

When I finally had the smarts to take myself to the doctor, it turned out I had a parasite infection. So, if anybody wants to lose a lot of weight really fast, I would suggest a parasite infection. It will really do it for you, but the cure is almost as bad as the sickness.

I would see people afterwards and women would say, "What have you done to lose the weight?"

I said, "Well, I haven't done anything but I've been invaded by a parasite."

One of my friends said, "Pardon me, but when you are through with him may I have him?"

I said "Gladly, with my blessing you may have him, but you'll have to take the Flagil that goes with it, which is the medication and it is really awful."

So things were going from bad to worse to even worse as a result of all that was happening. The actual funeral itself, however, was a wonderful celebration of who Larry was. It didn't make him out to be perfect because perfect he wasn't. But it made him out to be the human being he was, and that was plenty good enough. We had a private gravesite ceremony with maybe a 100 or 150 people, which was appropriate because I would have been overwhelmed with that many for the actual burial.

After one has done what you need to do with the burial of a loved one, and in my tradition, after one has sat Shivah, people go home. People need to go home, they have lives; they have obligations, responsibilities. They need to go on with doing what they need to do.

Then you are alone, you are really, really alone.

It's the kind of aloneness that I had never experienced before. It's the kind of aloneness I would never have chosen to experience ever in my life. It isn't just that there is no one there to talk to; it's that the person you shared everything with, the person who mattered most is no longer there.

This was the person with whom you had created a personal history, the person to whom you looked, with whom you could exchange a glance, knowing you didn't have to say anything; you knew what that person was thinking or communicating. The person you shared dreams with, the person you planned the future with and for; he is not there and is not replaceable. And he isn't going to be there. Every night at 7:00 I would wait for the door to open, and every night at 7:00 nothing.

Heartbeats

- Make deposits in your memory bank so you can withdraw them later when you need them.
- Don't miss an opportunity to tell people how much you love them and what they mean to you.
- Whatever your faith or tradition, use it, you'll need it.
- See a doctor, you'll be dysfunctional in ways that are normal but scary.
- Claim your own pain, you pay now or you pay later.
- Get counseling, if only to have a listener who can reassure you.
- Don't canonize your departed one, it dehumanizes them and is unfair.
- The emptiness will take a very, very long time to get over.

Now the Hard Part

CHAPTER 4

There are stages of grief that everyone is familiar with by now. At this point in my life, I was angry, I was enraged. How could you do this to me? How could you leave me like this? How could you make me face the worst possible situation of my whole life alone? Any other time when something awful had happened or something painful had happened or something even problematic had happened, we'd always shared this, you'd been there for me. How could you make me face this alone now? How could you leave me? How could you leave all of the dreams and the hopes we had for the rest of our lives together, dreams to retire to this fabulous house we'd just finished in Ireland? How could you do this to me? How could you leave? How could you just up and go?

In my mind, the easy part was the dying. You just closed your eyes and went to sleep; that was the easy part. The living was the hard part, the keeping on going every single day when you really had not a whole lot of reason to keep going or much incentive to keep going. That was the hard part, and I was angry with him for doing that. I was angry with him for leaving me. I was angry with him for dying too soon. I was angry with him for not taking proper care of his health, which he had neglected because he just didn't think it was going to be that important. And I was really angry with God. Where was God when all of this went on?

Now this is a pretty internalized and fairly egocentric sort of a thing; after all, where was God during the holocaust? But I wasn't dealing with the holocaust just at this moment, I was dealing with my pain and my loss and my husband, and where was God in all of this? I am not sure yet if I have figured out where God was. If that sounds blasphemous then thus be it, but I wasn't very happy with

15

God; I was very angry, and the day of the funeral the rabbi asked me how I was doing and I said I was angry. I'm angry at my husband's death and I'm angry at God. He said to me, you have a reason to be angry and a right to be angry, and God owes you a reckoning. I am so grateful that he said that because had somebody, anybody said to me, "Well, these things happen, and God knows best or this is God's will," I probably would have become absolutely homicidal.

As time wore on, I gradually, very, very gradually, and only incrementally, began to come to some peace, to a realization that it isn't because you are a person of faith that you are spared these tragedies in life. And it isn't because you believe God will look out for you or that bad things will not happen to you because bad things do happen to good people. What the faith provided for me was not an insurance policy that I would never get hurt, it was the possibility of a coping skill, something that would allow me to reach down into myself and pull myself up by the radical roots of my belief. Something that would give me the strength and the courage and whatever it took to go forward, knowing that in the midst of the worst of life, life is good . . . life itself is very good. I clung tenaciously, and do to this moment cling tenaciously, to the belief that life, even when it is not so hot, is very good and very, very precious because there is nothing to replace it, there is no substitute.

About a month or maybe six weeks after my husband's death, and I always use the term death, and I say that he died. I don't say he's passed, I don't say he's gone to another life, I don't say that he is whatever. I say that he's dead, and he died, and he's gone for good because I need to know in my own mind the finality of that. It isn't that he's passed over some place, and maybe he'll just pass back. He is dead, and he is gone. About six weeks or so after that, I began to have very vivid and for me sort of peculiar dreams.

I'm, unfortunately, not one of those people who remembers dreams in the morning, so the fact that I can remember and recount this is in itself rather remarkable. I had a dream that I was standing and could see Larry at a distance. In my dream I felt this gush, almost a river of water flowing through me and past me and on to the other side of where he was. In this water I could see episodes of our life and moments that we had shared. They were like living pictures that were flowing in this river. I felt as if I were being eviscerated, as though my guts were coming out with all that was happening, all of this extraction of all of this water.

At the end of the dream I was still alive, and that was an amazing feeling to me, so I began to think about what this could mean to me? Well, I very much believe in goddess symbolism, and I knew that for me this flowing, this river, was a birth symbol, a giving birth. I had done that many times, and I am familiar with what that feels like. In a sense, it was like giving birth not only to his death but giving birth to myself in the new life I was going to have to somehow establish. It was a cleansing in a sense, a renewal, a washing away of that which had been ours, but it wasn't a drowning of it. He was still on the other side of this river and I was on my side. He was where he was, and was okay, and I was where I was and in time I would be okay. That was a very important symbol for me.

I would eventually have moments when I would see him or I would hear him, and that's pretty spooky. I would be waking, usually in those sort of half life moments when you're a little bit awake, a little bit asleep. My husband would often get up in the morning and go and work at the computer, and he would find something that he thought was going to be of great interest to me on the Internet. He would print it out and walk across our bedroom past me in bed and say, "I found this for you on the web, and I am going to put it by your sink because I think you'll find this interesting."

He often did this in his underwear, a sight to behold, and I had visions of him doing this again. I could hear him, and it was so vivid I would get up and go into my dressing room to look for the things he had left for me. That, I am told, is not an indication I'm totally going crazy but a fairly typical thing that happens to people who are bereaved. I also had moments when I would hear him laughing at a joke, a story that he really loved or a piece of music that he really enjoyed. I could hear his voice saying something to me. His nickname for me was Soshie because my Hebrew name is Soshana. I could hear him saying, "Come on Soshie, let's go," and it was as if I could turn on a dime, and he would absolutely, positively be there.

I was asked by my therapist, "How did he look?" He looked good, actually; he looked okay. In my mind I wasn't seeing him in the last stages of his illness in which he looked so awful and so unlike himself. Yes, I did wake up at times, and I would have that image vividly imprinted on my memory, but not so much anymore. Now I was seeing him as he was, full of life and full of vigor, watching him take great delight in something that one of the grandchildren had done. Or, when I'm in Ireland, I expect any moment to see him come through the door and tell me he's just been hiking through what I guess we could refer to as the back forty, to tell me what he's seen and what he's found and who's done what. He would always tell me the latest story on all the neighbors, etc. Of course, I miss that terribly, but it's very, very real, so there is this sense in my mind that wherever he is, he is okay.

The last week of my husband's life we were in Ireland, where he loved to be more than any place. He may have had a premonition that something was wrong, more so than he was letting on, because I heard him say to both our general contractor, a wonderful man, and to the farmer from whom we had purchased our property, "Pat and Joe, if anything happens to me, be sure you look after Suzanne," which was strange because no one was expecting anything to happen.

This was February, and Larry was expecting us to return to Ireland the 21st of March. Oddly, or sadly, he died on the 20th of March.

He also had said to the man who did the interior colors in this house, a very talented person, "Sean, this may be the last time you ever see me." I only know that because Sean told an American friend of ours, and he relayed the information to me.

Then, as we were driving through the Caha Pass back to Shannon and to the airport, something amazing happened. This mountain pass is probably the one spot on earth that thrilled my husband most. This was his spot, this was his personal heaven. It had rained, as it certainly does in Ireland, and there was a rainbow across the valley. He stopped the car and took pictures of the rainbow. As we were driving he said to me, "You know Suzanne, if something were to happen to me, I think you should make a life for yourself; at least half of your time in Ireland.

I said, "What is all of this business about something happening to you? Where is all of this coming from?"

He said, "I don't know, I've just been thinking that this would be a good thing for you to do."

As of this writing, I am trying to do that which he thought would be a good thing for me. He is right, and I am trying to find my way and find my place.

It was in Ireland that he really got in touch with the spiritual and the mystical part of himself. I suspect this is why it is here that I feel his presence so much. As I drove for the first time since his death through the mountains and through this valley, through this mountain pass, thinking about the deep coma he was in the days before he died, I just knew where he was. I felt his spirit was hovering somewhere in this valley. Then, when I came around this one mountain with its spectacular view of Bantry Bay, I had to stop the car and pull over because I was overcome with weeping, with the palpable feeling that this was where my husband was.

If there's a heaven for him, this has to be it.

That was very difficult, that first trip to Ireland. Walking in the house was not as hard as I thought it might be because, in order to get this house finished, I had made this trip by myself many times. So I was used to coming here by myself and walking into the house by myself. What was very painful was the first night in Ireland after Larry died, sleeping in our bed. Larry had gone directly from the airport to the hospital in Houston and never went home to sleep in our bed. The last place we had slept together was in our bed in Ireland. Because we were only here for five days, I decided not to change the sheets. We would be back in a month, there was no need. There is a smell everybody has, each of us has our own personal aroma, and I could smell his cologne and his presence in those sheets and in that bed. That was very hard, that was a painful time, and I didn't sleep particularly well the first night. Actually, I slept very little the first night, but it got better. Meeting each of these hurdles face on and not putting them off, I think, has been better than doing it some other way.

Shortly after my husband died, within a couple of weeks, was Passover, and that was awful. We had always enjoyed large Passover celebrations, maybe 25 people. I just could not be in that house and see that empty dinning room, knowing my husband would not be leading a Seder this year, or any other year for that matter. We will have other Seders but it will be pretty raw for me for a long time to come. This first time, however, I went to Austin and had Seder with my daughter Kathryn's family, and that was helpful.

That first Mother's Day without him also was very difficult because Larry always did something special and fun for me on Mother's Day. Then came my birthday in May. I went to New York to see my parents. I wanted to see my parents. They were not capable of making the flight to Houston for Larry's funeral, and I am sure, as a parent myself, they were terribly concerned about me, about how I was holding up. And I needed to see how they were doing to reassure myself it was okay for me to perhaps leave the country again soon. I needed to be someplace besides Houston for my birthday because my last birthday had been my 60th, and we'd had this big, big party, and I knew I would be thinking about that and the wonderful pictures we'd taken, and so on.

Then came Father's Day. It was painful, too. There is no father, no patriarch for our family, no paterfamilias any more. We have a granddaughter, Lauryn, born six days after Larry died whom he will never know. We have other small grandchildren who are too young to remember. Emily, Jonah, Noah and Nicholas who intuitively knew something was wrong but were too little to explain the situation to. We have grandchildren on the way that will never know him, and that is such a loss. That is such a loss for him, and it's such a loss for them. He was a larger than life figure, and they will never have anybody in their life like that.

The next big event for me was my husband's birthday in July. I didn't want to be at home in Houston for that either. The months of June and July would be my first trip back to Ireland. I needed to be in Ireland for Larry's birthday because we had never been here together for his birthday. I wasn't going to have to relive those memories again. That was helpful.

The next things that come along are the Jewish Holiday's. There will be no anniversary, Thanksgiving, Hannuka or New Year's. We were in Ireland last year for New Year's so I don't know if that's something I can handle or not. It will sort of depend on how far along I am in the grief process. But I do know that there are certain things that have helped me and that may be of help to somebody else.

On the subject of advice, I will say this: The advice I received from others was generous, gratuitous and for the most part worthless. The only people who, interestingly enough, have little advice to offer are the people, women particularly, who have been where I am because they know you have to walk your own walk, and nobody can do it for you. You can just be there for them, invite them for dinner or whatever. By the way, when invited to something, go. Get dressed and go because the longer you put off doing these things the harder it becomes. It would be fairly easy to stay in your house in your bathrobe and that's it. But doing so is just postponing. It's like having an open wound that you refuse to let be stitched. The longer you ignore it, the worse it can become.

The best advice I have for somebody who might be walking in these shoes is to locate reliable people and use them. Find a good counselor. Talk to somebody. Have somebody available to whom you can vent your fears, your angers, your resentments, your despair, knowing that this is a safe thing to do, that you are not keeping it all bottled up. Don't clutch those negative feelings to your bosom and cling to them dearly because they will eat at you like a true viper. You need to air them and get them out and get rid of them and move on. It is a time when there will be lots of people who will be giving you advice about what to do with your property, what to do with your financial resources.

Be very wary of those folks. Find good advisers, people in whom you have faith and confidence and trust, and go with them. A good attorney, a good accountant, financial planner or financial advisor – those are the things you will need. You don't need your great uncle from wherever coming along and telling you, "Oh, you should invest in this."

People will call you and solicit you, and you will drown in the mail. They will send you so much information advising you to invest in this or put your money here. You are a very vulnerable person at this point in every way. It is most important that you be aware of your own vulnerability and be very, very cautious about what you do with any of your resources.

Heartbeats:

• Be angry at what happened but eventually give yourself permission to move on.

• There is no set schedule for grieving even though there are phases; shock, denial, depression, anger and acceptance.

• A major point; how long you grieve does not reflect how much you loved.

• All firsts will be very painful.

• No, you don't know how I feel.

• Be weary of anyone who wants to "help you with your assets," they'll crawl out of the woodwork. Good people are available; use them.

• You are very vulnerable. Make as few major decisions as possible for at least a year.

First Steps the Most Difficult

CHAPTER 5

To our great dismay, my husband and I had not finished our estate planning. We were in the process and had scheduled to complete it in the spring. He died before that was done. He had not given durable power of attorney to anyone, which only complicated life immeasurably. His will and his business arrangements were not complete . . . It was all very complicated, it was convoluted. That ends up punishing the very people you hope to leave things to and provide for.

I would encourage anyone at any age to get an attorney, to get a will and a power of attorney, and to make any physicians directives known. Let a doctor know what you want – this Larry did do – and what you don't want done in the event you are in the condition my husband was in because you don't want things to linger and linger and linger, for yourself or for your family. It is a time when you go from meetings with attorneys to accountants and back to court. It feels as though each day you're just getting dressed, wound up, and having to sit through another long arduous meeting or go to another court presentation or whatever. It's not an easy time, it's a time you have to get through, a time when you are very vulnerable.

It's also a mixed blessing. You're busy, and the busyness of it means you have to get up and get going. The down side is it would be very easy and frankly very tempting to just deal with the busyness and business of it and not to deal with the emotional part. To grieve and achieve at the same time is a really tall order, and I am not sure many of us are able to do that, but that is certainly almost what's expected of you when something like this happens. I have been told by professional therapists and by friends, people who love me, that I'm being very brave.

That is a very flattering thing to hear, and empowering to have it recognized and acknowledged that you're bucking up and you're doing what you need to do, carrying on with dignity, etc. But underneath all that, I feel very little and very scared and very alone a lot of the time. I need to know the real skinny of what's going on in my life, and I need to be able to share that with certain people, not with everybody.

By the way, after about two months, people have definitely lost interest in hearing about your sad stories. People will sympathize and empathize with you for a couple of months, not because they don't care or not because they're disinterested, but because people have their own life, their own grief or *tsuris* as we say in Yiddish. Simply stated, you are not the center of everybody else's universe. Your own universe is so imploded you can't see beyond. Trust me, other people have problems, and other people are only going to listen to your problems just so long, and then they will begin to avoid you.

I had made the decision early on that I did not want to be avoided. I didn't want to be abandoned. I didn't want to be left alone by friends and associates. The only way to escape this was not to be a wet blanket every place I went. So you put on your happy face, and you get yourself up and go do what you have to do. And repetitive as that seems, it's the kind of a pep talk you need to give yourself over and over and over again because it's just kind of the way it is.

I am not the center of anybody else's universe and/or concerns, including our children to whom I said, "Look, you have been wonderful but it is time now for you to go about your own business. You have your own lives, your own kids, your own spouses, you have got to get on with your own lives, and I'm giving you permission to do that, I'm encouraging you to do that. Your career, your job in life is not to baby-sit mother. I am going to have to get on by myself. Do I want you to check out on me, never talk to me or see me? Certainly not. I want to be included, and I want to be part of everything and kept apprised of what you are doing and where you are going and so on, but I am not your principal concern. Your principal concern is each other and your own children."

I think that was a good thing to do for them and it was important to do for me. Having said all of that, it is necessary to acknowledge, because it sure is the truth, that the evenings are always difficult, and it's worse on the weekends. The weekends are usually couples time or family time. You're lonely and it's the pits.

Especially at the beginning, my phone would ring constantly. I would come back and the call notes would show 20 or 30 messages. That, of course, dwindled but still you get people calling and life goes on . . . except on the weekends. On the weekends you can go a whole day, a whole Saturday, Saturday evening, Sunday, Sunday evening and the phone won't ring. There is no one inquiring about you, no one inviting you to do something because you are the odd person out and because people have gone forward with their plans and their lives. They're not hovering over you anymore. That's the hardest part of the daily or weekly routine for me, the getting through the nights and weekends.

It gets better, though, because you plan things. You take a class, you teach a class, you go to a lecture. The weekends are really, really difficult because you are that third person, the odd person at a dinner party. You're in a world of couples, which was my world for all of my adult life. I am the odd person now and that's very, very hard. It takes a long, long time to get used to that. Maybe I will never get used to it, maybe it's just something that will always be a sad part of my life. It's almost impossible to visualize that I will ever be totally happy again.

Are there moments of happiness? Certainly there are. These are the special occasions such as the birth of grandchildren. There are special occasions in my life or in my children's lives or in the lives of my friends. But will there be happiness in the sense of contented peace, the stability of life, the security of loving and being loved? Probably not. That's an awful loss, that's a terrible, terrible loss. It's a chasm of loss actually, and I am not sure there is ever going to be a bridge or a lifeline that reaches that. It may be that I will just be forever standing at the abyss and looking into it and facing, "That's it. This is what is." I would have never, never signed up for this. Some people are happy being alone. They do well alone. I am not happy being alone. I'm doing as well as I can, and I'm probably doing okay, but I am certainly not happy to be alone.

There are obligations that will have to be met for anybody who is suddenly widowed, and you do those things. You hope your life will go forward in a lifestyle, not terribly significantly less then it was before. But that may not be the case. There will be expenses, there will be bills, and they will be turning up forever. You will say, thank God, I am finally through with all of this, I finally know where I stand financially, I finally paid off the last bill, and then you'll get another one from someplace.

The medical bills, for instance, will take a very long time to be settled. The business accounts will take a very long time to be worked through and to be settled. There were obligations in Ireland that could resurface a year or two after the event. When you think you're finally done and you've paid off the last debt and whatever, not so. So that is another jolt. And when you are on a fixed income, or suddenly on a fixed income, those are not happy jolts.

The realization, the preparation for these eventualities are definitely significant items to put in your little pile of "to do" notes. That is, be very cautious, be very conservative with your finances because you really don't know yet where you're going to stand or how many things you will be facing. It's tacky to think about having to deal with money when what you're dealing with is a broken heart. But the realities are such that you will have to deal with money, and you will have to deal with obligations you and your husband shared. You will have to somehow manage to provide for yourself the kind of financial security you'll need. I was widowed at 60. If I live to be an old woman, I need to know I will have the financial resources to provide me with a decent lifestyle and to provide for my care in my old age. This is why you must be sure you have a corpus you don't dip into because, should you become very sick and elderly, there is no one to provide for you.

I had never had to do that, and this is a little late in the game to be on the learning curve. It is amazing how you do what you have to do because the choices are so stark. You either do it or you don't do it. But, if you don't do it, the results and the consequences are dreadful. So you just do what you have to do, and in some ways each day is a little bit better then the day before. At the same time, in other ways it will be worse. The post-Enlightenment mentality that every day and in every way you're going to get a little bit better is not true. It isn't true that every day things are a little bit better. Some days, things are much better. Then, the very next day, it can be awful. It depends upon some very small insignificant thing that strikes you. It may be something like cleaning out some of your spouse's personal effects and coming across something, a toothbrush, for example. This can really dissolve you.

When we had to sell Larry's car because it was owned by his

company and not yet paid for – and I didn't need two cars anyway – selling the car wasn't so bad. But taking his golf clubs out of the car was awful, a very painful moment. I knew he'd never use these clubs again. That was it. They would go into storage or somebody else would use them, but he would never use them again. The garage has just my car in it now, so when I open it, and it's just my car, that emptiness, that just plain emptiness, stares me in the face.

Even for the month that he was in the hospital and the month afterward, before we sold the car, I knew he wasn't going to come back and drive the car, but it was there, it was his, it was a physical, tangible reminder of him. It was gone now, the car was gone. Other things similar to that will happen, and little by little you begin to feel denuded of your history, of your life together, of the things that were the person you loved, because they're gone. Some of that becomes economic necessity. Some of it becomes, I suppose, a matter of practicality. Whether you empty closets and drawers and things, I guess, is a personal decision. I opted to keep many, many things belonging to my husband until I felt ready. It will be a long time before I'm ready to let other things go, some things I will never let go.

I could go into his closet, and frankly it was comforting for me to see those were his things. They had his smell on them, I could touch them, they were things that had been on his body, and that was a solace to me, a comfort I was not willing to forgo until I was very, very sure I was very, very ready. There were personal items that I wanted my grandchildren to have so I put them in the safety deposit box. When the time comes, those things will go to the grandchildren or the children, but at a later time.

There is this temptation to rush to judgment about getting rid of things because it may seem too hard not to. Don't do that. The things that may seem hard to you at the moment may be of great comfort to you later. One night, as I was going through a lot of paper work, looking for insurance papers I came across some letters we had exchanged. My husband had saved those things.

He saved everything, and that was kind of nice. I sat in bed and surrounded myself with these mementoes. I made a little circle, and I felt a sense of love and a remembrance of when we were younger, of the passion and what that had been like for us. I was very grateful to have those things and to create those moments for myself. It is a coping skill that worked for me. It perhaps wouldn't work for everyone, but it was a very helpful thing to be able to surround myself with things that were special to us and have deep meaning. Those are things I have no desire to relinquish, particularly early on in the grieving process.

Heartbeats:

• The busyness of the business you'll have to do will help get you going; don't let it overwhelm you.

• Make friends with yourself, you'll need you.

• Only part with what you want when you want.

• Cry when you need to, talk when you need to and allow yourself to be quite as you need to.

The Fear Factor

CHAPTER 6

*E*arlier, I spoke about fear becoming a constant companion. The worst fear, of course, was that Larry would die, and then he did. The wound was raw, the wound was not healing, and the worst fear certainly transpired. I was in what I later would understand to be a kind of shock. I wasn't terribly afraid of my future, I was simply coping with the necessities that one has to cope with when suddenly faced with the loss of a spouse.

After about eight weeks, however, the numbness began to wear off, and new fears began to surface. I became afraid for my future. I became afraid that the advice I was being given and the people I was relying on were going to make mistakes. I had so much responsibility for an estate, a business, and decisions for which I was not prepared, nor had I anticipated at such a stage of my life, that I was terribly afraid. I was afraid I would make mistakes, and these would be costly mistakes to me and to other people. I was afraid for my future. I was afraid that I would not be okay, that I would not be secure.

I understood there would be certain changes in my way of life, obviously. But now, all of a sudden, I was going to be facing my old age and my older age without anybody to be my companion, without anybody to hold my hand, without anybody to be there for me in a way only a spouse can be there. I was afraid I was too young to pack it in and too old to start over. I was afraid that I would never feel again, and I was more afraid that perhaps some day I would. I felt the fear as a gnawing away at my innards. I got through days because I was busy. I got through the time because I had things I had to do of necessity.

Those were not the things compensating me for what was missing in my life. I was afraid I would make hasty decisions on certain things so I tried to be as circumspect and as calm and as judicious about decisions I would make as possible. But some decisions simply couldn't wait. Some decisions had to be made in the immediate future. I was afraid of my todays, and I was afraid for my tomorrows. I didn't know how to go on with my life, I didn't know who I was going to be now. I didn't know that I'd want to be anybody different than what I had been, but I knew that I was going to have to be.

I was worried that I would become a burden at some point to my family because as you age you have other kinds of needs and other kinds of concerns. I was worried about healthcare. I was worried about everything. Those are pretty natural enough fears and worries, I expect. And they were certainly interfering with my ability to go forward with my life and with my healing.

Soon, I found the healing to be a very erratic kind of experience. Some days I felt pretty good, at least I felt pretty good for parts of some days. Some days I felt the majority of the day desperate and lonely. The aloneness, the loneliness, and the fear of increased loneliness was enough to make me think, "Is this all my life is going to be for the rest of my life, however long that may be?" When faced with these kinds of gloom and doom thoughts, I would try to give myself a pep talk and say, "Don't project into your future, you can't project into the future." I could never have projected this part of my future so why borrow trouble I don't have.

Many, many years ago I had a secretary from Guatemala, and she had a wonderful expression that was, "Don't sweat another's fever." She was right. Why should I worry about things at this point, things over which I have no control and a future about which I knew nothing. It was easier said than done. As I would be out and about with other people or friends or acquaintances, or even among total strangers, and see how they took the mundane ordinariness of life so for granted – as had I – I wanted to scream at them, "Don't do this! It's so precious, every moment is so special."

Sitting over a cup of coffee in the morning with somebody you really love and who really is your partner is the kind of thing you only miss and appreciate when you no longer have it. Maybe that's one of the great ironies of life, that you really only appreciate that which you no longer have.

It was very hard to let go of what I had and who I was in order to deal with what I have and who I need to become. We all probably do this eventually in our own way. One of the things that worked for me was that I was very slow to get rid of the things that belonged to my husband. I was absolutely trenchant about refusing to get rid of things that were ours, things we had collected over a lifetime. Oddly enough, they brought me comfort, and they brought me a sense of peace and a piece of continuity, which I needed because my life had been so wrenched apart.

Part of the fear, I think, in looking back at that time was that there was always another shoe to be dropped, there was always another bill to be paid; there was always another unexpected glitch in the business. There was always something, and it never seemed to be good news facing me when I just about thought I had it all under control. So I lived with this anticipation that there was going to be more to come, and the more-to-come was not going to be good news because, frankly, nothing that had happened since Larry became sick turned out to be anything but bad news.

Living with this kind of uncertainty takes a toll. You pay a price for that sort of thing. It doesn't really allow you to get on with what you need to do or what I felt I needed to do. So maintaining the contact, the tangible physical contact with the things that were his and had been ours, was a comfort to me. It was my nightlight, my teddy bear. It was the thing that helped me to get through the days and more importantly the nights.

For me, part of the process of letting go, which I knew I had to do, was to go back and be in places where we had been, and where we had been very happy. In my situation, it was to return to Ireland, to the house we'd built there, the house that was our dream house, our retirement hope. The last week of my husband's life had been there. The first time coming back to Ireland was, I knew, going to be at best a bittersweet moment. The flight over was very, very easy, which was a gift because often times it's not. The first night, I stayed outside of Limerick with friends I'd known since my first trip to Ireland. I really needed to see them before I went down to the house. Then came the moment when I took the car and was making the drive from the airport area to our house, which is a good three-hour drive if you are moving right along, and there is not a lot of traffic.

The last day we were in Ireland, before he went to the hospital, there was a beautiful rainbow over the pass, and he stopped and took pictures and loved that view and loved that location.

There is a wonderful little song that the Muppets have about the rainbow connection. I guess I will always think of him as being my rainbow connection to the mountains and to the Cana Pass. Getting through the mountain pass and driving then down the coast road to our house was a very emotional moment. Fortunately, the sun was shining, there were no rainbows, so I didn't have to relive that experience just then. When I walked in the house, however, it was okay. It was just obviously the way I had left it.

The woman who looked after the house while we're gone was sure that everything was in order. I opened the house and checked on everything, and everything was fine. It felt okay. It felt like a good place to be. I had been here many times by myself in the process of getting this house completed and had actually lived here when it was finished for a few weeks before Larry had been able to come over in the previous summer.

I knew what it was like to be alone in this house. I was up all night. I was listening to the winds and the *baaaah* of the sheep in the meadow next door and wondered if this had been such a great idea. But then, little by little, my friends from America who were here, my friends from Ireland who were here, called on me and invited me to dinner. We went to a music event, and they afforded me just the right amount of company. It was enough company so that I wouldn't have to sit around desperate, but I had enough space so that I could do the grieving I needed to do.

In addition to the personal healing I was hoping would occur for me here, I had the business end of properties and bank accounts and home insurance, etc., in Ireland much the same as in America. All of that needed to be handled, and I still had work crews doing outside work.

Please God, they will someday finish with the outside work.

Little by little that is taking place. When I say little by little, I mean by tiny little increments even though lorries full of stones and dirt are being brought in to fill in the spaces in the back of the house. It is taking a mighty long time. Being an American and being an efficient American, I keep wanting to have it done and wanting to have it finished and completed and tidied up. The Irish keep saying to me, "in God's good time, in God's good time," or "in the fullness of time, in the fullness of time." I wish that God in his fullness would move on with getting my projects taken care of. Maybe I'll learn something about life here in that there is a fullness of time and a goodness of time. The only thing that probably changed the way I'm able to view the world and myself and my place in it is ultimately time and the experiences that time and only time will afford me.

Every sunny day is such a blessing, a benediction, really. When I look out at the ocean and back at the mountains, and I feel the wind in my face, and the air is so clean and pure, and I can stand here and scream and holler, and I can cry or do whatever, I'm so very grateful I have these freedoms.

That is a wonderful catharsis. When I walk this land and pick my own wildflowers and, in the fall, my own blackberries, there is such a sense of rootedness and connectedness to earth and to life that I only get here. I badly need this because part of what is so disconcerting: there is a level at which I know I'm functioning very well. I keep hearing this from people who are dealing with other folks in similar situations. "Oh, you're doing so well, you're doing so well."

That's good, that's better than not doing so well. But, it is as if I am a dual existent person because I feel I am floating around through the whole of my experience, a disconnect between what I am doing and what I perceive myself as doing.

I'm trying desperately to stay in touch with the things I feel, the good things, the not so good things, the pain that is my own, the loss, the depth of the loss, the loneliness. I know that, if I don't get in touch with those things, I'll only be suppressing them and sitting on a volcano that will come back to erupt and haunt me at a much later time, when I really don't need that.

Yet, there is something in my personality that doesn't permit me to let those things overcome me because then I would become immobilized. That's just not my way of coping.

So I do feel a kind of anomie. There is something that isn't totally in sync. Being a synchronized person, being a person who is grounded in realities, in faith and in experience has always been very important to me, so I am feeling a little lost, and that's probably an okay thing. I'm feeling distant from all that I knew and really distant from all that I think I'm going to someday become.

Heartbeats:

• Afraid of todays and afraid of tomorrows, so take it one day at a time.

• Take time to enjoy the small gestures and the little things while you can, you'll miss them terribly when they are gone.

• Find a safe place where you can cry, scream or do whatever you need to let the pain and anger out.

• The disconnect between what you feel and how you function will eventually heal.

• Remember, your loved one died -- the love you shared did not.

New Realities

CHAPTER 7

*I*t's an odd age to be alone. If I were 40, I would be thinking in terms of a new life. I might think in terms of, perhaps, someday falling in love again and starting a new life. If I were 80, I would think in terms of just managing to maintain my health and my well being for the remaining years. But I'm 61. I'm too young to be simply on maintenance and too old to want to start all of this all over again. So what does one do with the rest of one's life? How do you pick up the pieces and make yourself feel valuable and useful? It's not that I was a dependent person on my husband for my sense of value or my sense of usefulness. I had achieved a lot in my own right and hopefully will continue to do so. But, the interdependence of somebody that I cared so for, and who is no longer there to share those moments with, is what makes it so difficult. It's almost as if the prize isn't worth having if there's no one to hug you and say, "Well done" and really be proud of you and appreciate what you have done.

These are the kinds of new realities that everyone widowed must deal with. Some people – and I am very observant now of people in this situation – some people rush to find somebody to take the place of the person they have lost. Nobody will take the place of a person you have loved and lost. Because of the personality of my husband, no one would ever take his place anyway. He was certainly a person who was larger then life in almost every way. He made himself known and his presence known every place he went, and had a magnetic type of personality that attracted people from all walks of life to him. He liked so many things and was interested in so many things. Even the things I was interested in and he wasn't, he became interested in because they were new and different, and that's the kind of mind he had.

So there won't be a somebody to replace him. I don't know that going about looking for that would be a particularly good thing to do. I don't think that trying to suddenly divorce myself from my home and my possessions and move into a new environment that's fresh and sterile and has no memories is a good thing to do either. In either case, I am concerned that, come a year from his death, when I have a better handle on the whole financial situation, which is now being dealt with on a month-to-month basis, I can then make better decisions. All of this is predicated on my staying healthy and functional and productive and all of those good things. That's hoping for quite a lot right at this point.

In addition, we have many, many children and grandchildren. I want to be an ongoing part of their lives and them to be an ongoing part of mine. I need to be able to be a fun grandmother, not the kind of grandmother who's weepy all the time and looking pitiful all the time. I don't want these to be the memories that are impressed on these children, many of whom will never have known their grandfather. They will have been born shortly after his death, or were so little at the time of his death that they will not have any memories. We have wonderful videos and pictures and etc. that can be played over to show children and to talk about. But, it's not the same as having somebody that can take your hand and show you how to do something wonderful like making things out of grass or doing things at the beach. They won't have those kinds of memories.

So I want to be the kind of grandmother for these children who can continue to supply not only my own memories for them but memories of their grandfather, some of which we will just have to relive over and over, and some of which we must create anew. In a sense, that is very life-renewing for me because it allows me to go on and live in the lives of my children and my grandchildren in ways that only this kind of continuity can permit you to do. In the Jewish tradition, one lives on in the memory of those who come after. So that memory connection and that memory bank we need to draw from for all of us is definitely terribly important for us personally and certainly as part of our tradition.

When I spent my first Friday night, my first Shabbat in Ireland alone and lit Shabbat candles and said the blessing over the wine, the Kiddush, and over the bread, the Hamotzi, I suddenly realized how many times we had done this. How many, many, many times we had done this so often mindlessly because it was Shabbat and it was what we did. Then I realized I was doing it by myself, for myself. That was a jolt, that was a reminder, again, that this was a new reality, a new way to experience life, a new way to express myself, not only in every other aspect but now religiously as well.

All of these firsts are things that have to be gotten through, and I know that. I wanted to be in Ireland for my husband's birthday because if he had a choice that's where he would have been for his birthday. His birthday was in July, so we had planned to be here; it was important to me to be here. If ever there was a place I was going to feel close to him, this would be the place.

Each of these firsts is very painful. Painful is a word that keeps repeating itself in my lexicon of descriptive words for what I'm going through. I often thought I had a fairly large vocabulary, but I find myself repeating the word "painful" over and over because in so many instances the situation is full of pain. There is no other way to get around it. The ownership of the pain has become almost a primal concern to me because I have watched so many people who don't take their pain seriously. They don't take it on, they just are numbed because they are taking medications or they're heavy duty into denial. The time would come when I would have to pay this awful debt, too, if I weren't dealing with it now.

This is not in anyway a choice of life people in their right mind would be making. I sit by my window and watch a circling greyback in the meadow in front of the Irish House, and I think of how free and floating and graceful that creature is, and I like to think this is the way my husband's spirit would be at this moment. I am very earthbound right now. I am very tied to the ground and to the earth and to heavy rock kinds of things because that's the way my heart is. I have this tremendous hole in my heart. My heart is empty, my bed is empty, it's not by any stretch of the imagination the way anybody would choose to live her life. It wasn't a choice that I was asked about, it was a situation I was given. The old adage about giving lemons states that you can do a number of things but the best possible thing, I guess, is to make lemonade. So this is what I am attempting to do with each of the things I face here.

Now, the dreams are becoming more vivid for me, too. I am not a person who usually remembers them. Some are happy dreams of times we had in the past, and some are dreams of times that were not so happy because I am allowing myself to let things surface that I would normally not want to think about because they would perhaps soil the memory of my husband and our marriage. But all of those are part and partial of who and what we were together. So it seems to me an allowable thing or at least a normal enough thing to say, Yes, some of the stuff I'm thinking about or remembering were difficult times. But, we got through them, and we survived them and were strengthened by them, and they were certainly real enough at the time, so it is not a big surprise they would be surfacing in my dreams.

Some of the things I find myself dreaming are things that would be fantasies of the future. Future moments that obviously won't happen. I fantasized about when we retired in a few years and spent months and months at this house in Ireland, and the things we would do, and the plans we had made, and the land we'd purchased would be taken care of, and it would look wonderful. We would be up and running with our computer equipment so we could work here as much as we'd choose to or as much as we would not choose to. How we would have made connections in the nearest city and know the good restaurants and where to go to purchase certain things and when good theater was coming and when the Jazz festival was coming, all of those things, and we would be able to enjoy those things. How we would drive to Cork and take the train into Dublin for a weekend of theater and shopping. All of these are things that we talked about and dreamed about and planned for.

In my dreams, sometimes we're doing these things and loving them. Of course, dreams are just that, and when you awaken you realize that those particular dreams, shared dreams, will not be shared. If they happen they'll happen because I do them by myself. That is certainly not the way the dream was suppose to end.

The crossover between my real life, my fantasy life and my dream life is sometimes a little bit blurred but only now because I am beginning to remember things I dream that I didn't use to remember.

Sometimes I wake up crying and can't even remember at first why. Sometimes I wake up very buoyant, not often, but once in a while. Again, sometimes I can't even remember why. I must have been thinking or feeling something really happy or really good at the time. It's not easy to share with friends and family on an ongoing basis what is going on in you because it is important to remember, at least it is important for me, to remember that people's sympathy and empathy only last just so long. Everybody has a life to which they are fully entitled, and everybody has their own sorrow, their own grief.

I am not the center of anybody else's universe. One of the many things you miss when you're widowed is that nobody is the center of anybody's universe except their own. You come in a close second to somebody who is your partner and is your spouse. Nobody else really will know or care about or take joy or sorrow in certain things. Nobody knows the little things that I miss. It's not the big things, it's the little stuff that I really miss so terribly. My husband knew me as a hummer. I hum and I don't even realize it. I hum when I do all kinds of things. When I'm angry or getting angry, I hum pieces from *Peter and The Wolf.* Only he would know that, and frankly only he would care. It was always a clue for him that something was amiss with me when I would be sitting next to him or in the car or in the kitchen or wherever and start humming the *Peter and the Wolf* tunes. That was a sign that things weren't so good with me, and I was probably about to blow.

Another thing he would know and care about is the fact that I have a problem with my colon, and sometimes it acts up and is painful. When that happens, I tend to be very quiet. So If we're sitting in a car, driving along, and I'm not talking and unusually quiet, he would look over and ask, "Is your colon bothering you?" Nobody else would know that, nobody else would frankly care about that. Nobody else would know that there are certain kinds of music I like and certain kinds of dancing I like to do. Just the everyday stuff, just the way you like your coffee, the way you eat, the way you sit a certain way. All of those are the kinds of things that only a lifetime of a shared history can provide. Those are the things I miss. I miss knowing he will know those things and care.

On the other hand, I miss the happy face that pops in the door, the sound of the voice, the chords, the new chords. He was always finding new chords on the piano. Listen to this, listen to these sounds. I've just found a new chord. The interest in all kinds of music and theater and philosophy and art and all of the things that Larry and I had shared, those are the kinds of things you just can't share with somebody else.

I even miss – I never thought I would live to say this – I even miss seeing him reach for his cell phone. He was probably the first human with an implant of a cell phone or cell chip in his head. He lived on the phone, his life was conducted on the phone, his stocks were done on the phone, his business was done on the phone. Everything was done on the phone. He was a person of great impulse, which was good and bad. Part of the impulse was, if he was thinking about somebody, regardless of where in the world they were, he would just pick up his cell phone and call them.

I have a strong suspicion that when Larry died, AT&T went into a grieving mode because they had lost one of the most prominent customers they will ever, ever have. There isn't anybody else we can now joke about as we did about Larry and his phone. Even if we were at our home in Ireland where you can't get good cell reception inside, he'd be outside in the wind talking. All of us who would be at dinner would be laughing about him being out on his phone. It used to annoy the hell out of me, but I would give an awful lot to be annoyed in that way today.

The things that connected me to the life we had created and to a solid foundation have eroded as shifting sand under my feet. I know I'm walking gingerly through my life now and through what I need to do because I am not sure what it is I need to do or who I need to be or what I'm going to be when all of this begins to settle in.

I look at my parents who are in their mid-80's, and I am so envious of the fact that they not only have lived to this ripe old age but that they have been able to experience this much life together. I feel terribly cheated that I didn't get to do that. I was cheated, and my husband was cheated and our kids and grandkids were cheated.

But life isn't fair, as people are constantly reminded. So to dwell on the fact that I was cheated doesn't help because I can't get my hands around the throat of the cheater. I can't blame anybody or punish anybody or retrieve that from which I have been cheated, which probably brings me back to the Almighty and my sense of disaffection in many ways from God and from God's mercy and all of those wonderful things because I don't feel that God was exactly on deck here when things were going south.

I know enough theologically, I know enough spiritually, to know that the hubris of it all is to expect divine intervention in the laws of nature to prevent someone's illness from taking its natural course. There is a wonderful line from Beowulf that I'm paraphrasing as I'm remembering it, but it says, "The fates will do as the fates must do."

All of my adult life and as long as I can remember, even as a child, I had a personal relationship with God. It was rocky sometimes, but I always had a personal relationship with God. So I am personally angered and offended and disappointed that God would have allowed such a thing to happen to my husband and to me.

It's going to take a long time before I can say I am on cozy terms with the Almighty. I have, since this experience, gained such respect for holocaust survivors who I know have maintained their faith in light of what experiences they had and the catastrophes and the apparent absence of God in the camps. How those people can still have faith and still believe in God, to me, is an amazing human achievement. I do believe in God. I don't deny the existence of God. I am just having a real tough time at the moment feeling in tune with the Almighty. I am seeking spirituality and finding spirituality more in nature and natural phenomena than I am in some ethereal or even written word sort of religious material.

There is something very elemental about going into the ground of earth and water and air and trees and rocks that have their own spirit life that is so basic to the whole of human experience and the whole of created experience. That's kind of where I find I need to be right now. I can't go too much further or deeper than that because I tend to become unaffected by lots of text or aphorisms.

Fortunately, few people, probably because they see the look in my face of sheer horror, have said anything foolish to me like, "Someday you'll know the reason for this." I will never know the reason for this! There is no reason for this, this is the sort of thing where people say, "Shit Happens," and that's exactly the way this is. This is God's will? What kind of God wills these kinds of things on people? If this is what God does, then I don't want to be too friendly with a God who wills things like this. The idea that somehow it's all for the best. . . . What kind of best? What sort of a best could this be?

Is there a pattern or reason or something I will discover at some later date? No, no, no! None of that! It's a loss, it's a pain, it's a wound, it's a gaping hole in my heart and in my life. The fact that it happened, I don't attribute to God's will, but there are moments when I would say a little indifference on the path of the Almighty might have contributed to some of this. This is not the theological meandering of someone who truly does not know better. It's just the cry of the heart to understand why such a presumably loving God would permit a loving human being and a person much loved by family and friends to depart this world in such an untimely manner while the nasty and the evil and the cruel of the world seem to prosper and go on forever?

The perennial problem of evil is certainly not new to me or to this experience, but it has been rejuvenated in a very, very personal and a very, very particular way by dealing with this death at this time.

Heartbeats:

• Much as people may love you, their empathy and sympathy only last so long.

• Life isn't fair; I was cheated, my husband was cheated and our family also. There comes a time when you have to say, "This is where I am now and this is where I have to go."

• Dreams may be very real and frightening, this too will level off in time.

• If you believe in God, you will be very angry at God right now. Both you and God can survive the strain.

• Keep in mind being or staying stuck has its own payoff, being walled off and feeling guilty if you laugh or have a good time, if you continue this, the payoff is it feels good to be punished because that's what you feel you deserve. This is not healthy grieving.

The Next Phase

CHAPTER 8

I have passed the heart-wrenching, sobbing phase and now weep gently, easily and often. Hearing a great jazz riff or seeing the face of a new grandchild or the unintentional touch of a stranger in the supermarket can make my reservoir of sadness spill over. God forbid I should speak in clichés or, even worse, become one.

Yet, the pain of loss is an ever-present reality. Getting through each day is a victory. Some people need to withdraw into themselves at first. Some of us are more active. Then comes the time when there is only you in your reality. Now, how beautiful everything here looks. It was, of course, always so, but confronted with death and the unknown number of tomorrows, the beauty is piercing.

Why didn't I take more time to just look and really see? Why does anybody harbor minor hurts or grudges when so very little really matters? Living on the knife-edge between life and death does tend to clarify one's thinking. Eventually, this too will become "normal" but for now there's an instinctive hunger, an insatiable hunger to drink in every living thing – the water, the trees, the lambs and the hares that keep me company, the mountains that change by the hour . . . it was all here before me and will be so long after I'm gone.

For now, the only way I can truly handle this is like a wailing saxophone that has tight harmony, all so tentative that I don't want to miss a minute despite the hurt. As Pippin says, "Without a hurt the heart is hollow."

But where does it reside, this will to go on? Is it merely the instinctive drive to live, to perpetuate life? Is it because I'm still feasting on my memories and because my memories are fresh and ever present? Is that what gives me the initiative, the drive to go forward? Is it something in a faith dimension, a spiritual dimension that enables you to say, "No matter how horrible this is, I can somehow and will somehow get through this?"

There is a wonderful Steven Sondheim song that talks about a woman who has seen good times and bad times but is still here. Perhaps that is where the will to go on resides, in that resiliency of knowing I had great times and now I'm having bad times, and I was there in the good times and I'm somehow still here in the bad times. There is a sense that some part of the essential me is irrevocably changed. At first, I was frantically and furtively trying to get that back. I wanted back what I had, and I wanted, most of all, I wanted my husband back and our life back. Since I couldn't have that, I operated out of a sense that, if I could just get the part of me back that had been severed or damaged or lost, somehow I could begin to become more whole. My life would somehow return to a normalcy.

Part of me is not coming back, so I am perplexed as to where is this reserve, this reservoir of strength that I'm finding? Thank God it's there, but what I'm finding is a deep recess, a deep well within me. It doesn't make it any easier, not by a long shot does it make it any easier. But it makes it possible, and it's the possibles–the "Yes, I could do this," or "Perhaps I could do that,"–that begin to give you a glimmer of a new life.

There are the musts, the things that have to be done, the shoulds, the oughts that will confront you when faced with being left alone, faced with being a widow, which is perhaps different than losing a parent or losing a child or losing a sibling.

When you lose your spouse and have financial considerations, properties and a business, and all the things that people accumulate and build together over a lifetime, you have obligations that for the most part cannot wait. So those are the musts and the shoulds that one has to do.

Then, little by minutia little, possibilities begin to assert themselves. Someone, after several months, may call and suggest a possibility, in my case such possibilities as, "Would you be interested in doing a workshop for us?" or "Would you be interested in teaching or at least co-teaching a class in a certain place?"

Those kinds of things are life-affirming because they make you think, and it gives you the sense that there are people who consider you to be a person of value in and of yourself. Intellectually, I certainly know that, but it's such a blow to your personal sense of wholeness and integrity, and a terrible blow, oddly enough, to your ego to be abandoned by the person you expected to grow old with. You begin to see yourself in a different light and in many cases a diminished light. By projection, you assume other people see you in the same way.

It is very empowering and reaffirming to have people present possibilities. Not earth shattering stuff – no one's suggesting the Nobel prize here – but the fact that somebody is making overtures that are intellectually challenging and would require a quid pro quo, after all they are going to pay you, is very rewarding. And they expect you to provide a service in return.

It's also somewhat scary because there is the possibility that I'm not up to it, that it will be more than I'm, frankly, capable of delivering. But you don't know until you try. Because people who are engaging your services know of your circumstance, or my circumstance, there's a presumption that they will be gracious, and I will give it, certainly, whatever I do, my best shot.

In the sixth month of the first year of my widowhood, which actually sounds almost Biblical, we had the gift of two new grandchildren join our family, a beautiful new grandson and a precious little granddaughter. Of course, each of these events is a mixed blessing because we look at these beautiful children and realize once again that these are children who will never know their "Pepa." These are children he will never know, children he will never have the pleasure of watching grow and develop. That is a very bitter sweet and a very sad and mixed blessing.

Also, by now, and I think perhaps this is a fairly common, fairly typical, I have certainly gone well past denial and have worked through a lot of the anger. Now I am feeling the sadness, the despair and the reality is very palpable. I try very hard not to project into my future and think, "Oh God, is it going to be like this forever and forever," because no one knows, of course, what forever is going to be. Certainly I would never had predicted a year ago that this is what my situation would be today.

For the first five or six months of being alone, I slept poorly. I slept, but not uninterruptedly and not for any great length of time. If I got six hours a night, that would have been a lot of sleep. Cumulatively, this eventually takes its toll, and by the fifth or sixth month of this, I began to experience real fatigue and a sense of tiredness. One of the things that worried me was the fact that I didn't want to slip into a form of unhealthy depression.

One of the symptoms, of course, of being depressed is either eating too little or too much, or having a change in sleep patterns. In this case, it would be an increase in the desire to sleep. I probably have more of an apprehension of this than many people might because my husband, in all his adult life, battled the demons of depression. He came from a family in which depression did not run in his family, depression galloped in his family. So this frightened him that he would end up being incapacitated by depression as had his own father.

People handle this in a variety of ways. Most of his life, until really the last couple years of his life, he kept his demons at bay by extreme exuberance, effervescence, boundless energy, lots of jokes, and lots of laughter. For all who knew him outside his immediate family, this was his public persona. As the Irish say, "He hung his fiddle at the door."

Eventually, however, he discovered that this really wasn't enough, and he finally sought medical help and got medical help, and it was a blessing. It was something that was manageable, and it was a healthy wholesome thing for him to do. But, having lived with someone who was always on the edge of giving in to depression, it is a very scary phenomenon to be a part of and to observe. So it's something that I have developed a healthy fear of and respect for simply because this was an experience I really acquired through being married.

I have perhaps an unreasonable fear that, if I'm tired and if I need to sleep more and if I am finding it difficult to get going in the morning, Oh, my God these are signs of depression, and we all know where that goes. However, I have the benefit of good counsel, both psychological and medical and am told it's probably just the fact that I'm so fatigued and just plain dead tired.

Now I have finally reached the point where my psyche and my body are saying, "Hold on girl. You've really got to slow down, you have just got to slow this pace." I am trying to do that and not be concerned about it in an undo manner. But it is disconcerting to me to think that I'm not bounding out of bed in the morning, that I'm sleeping later then I normally would sleep, and I'm falling asleep in the afternoon if I'm sitting quietly reading, and I know this is not my normal MO. However, as my kids want to remind me, "You're getting older Mother and older people do sleep more."

Maybe there is something to all of that. A few years ago the Queen of England referred to her particular year as an annus terribilis. Now, when Elizabeth spoke about this, she was speaking about the antics of her grown children and the disgrace and the grief they had brought upon the personage of the Queen. I, however, am not thinking so much about anything my kids have done or not done, I'm thinking of what a year this had been in the disarray my husband left.

Larry preached a wonderful game about financial responsibility. Unfortunately, he didn't live it in quite the same way he preached it. So we are unraveling and patching and making good a lot of financial things that probably we would not have had had he lived longer and been able to straighten them out himself. At the same time, this was the year the stock market took such a significant dive, and there was probably nothing he could have done to salvage the financial situation as he saw it or as it came to unfold.

In addition to all of that, this was the year people of diabolical intent took two loaded jets and flew them into the World Trade Center towers as well as into the Pentagon and into a field in Pennsylvania. This horror happened two days before the celebration of my wedding anniversary. I am not saying that the loss and the horror of what happened is in any remote way comparable to what I was feeling at this time, but what it did do was it reinforced the sense of loss.

Now I was seeing in living color, again, horror and nightmare and terrible, terrible loss. Fortunately, a psychiatrist was on television explaining to people that it's pretty normal to feel fear and anxiety and apprehension and all of the things that go with a phenomenon, an experience such as this. What it does, is to bring up, at least on a subconscious level, all of the losses you have experienced in your life: when the dog died, when your grandmother died, perhaps when your parents got divorced.

Whatever was a terrible loss for you at some point in your life becomes, in a sense, a scab that gets picked at again when something as horrific as this happens, and this kind of horrible human tragedy is unfolding daily and hourly in front of you.

I had hoped not to be in the States when my anniversary came along because I wanted to be someplace where we had not yet celebrated a wedding anniversary and we had not ever had an anniversary in Ireland so I had hoped to be there. Of all of the holidays, be they birthday, Mother's Day, Father's Day, Hanukkah, Thanksgiving, whatever, the one I dreaded the most was the celebration or observance of my wedding anniversary because that's just our day.

Other days were days we shared with other people and with family, friends, but a wedding anniversary is just that, it's the anniversary of the wedding of the two persons involved. So I had hoped to be someplace other then at home. This was the time in our history, however, when all commercial airline flights and many other kinds of flights were cancelled, so I was not able to be where I had hoped to be. I sat and I waited until the planes were able to fly. It was a very interesting experience to be on an airplane within a few days and flying overseas after the World Trade Center bombing.

Usually, the Houston airport is mobbed. I got there dutifully my two to three hours in advanced and walked straight up to the ticket counter, and I was it . . . there was no line. The connecting plane itself, however, was fairly well occupied because there were people who were heading home for Ireland who had been stranded for a week in the United States. The flight crew was about to board the plane when we were made aware that there was going to be a little delay, and you all know what little delays mean for an airplane, because they were going to make another security check. That does tend to get your attention after what had happened.

Once on board, however, the flight was very uneventful. It was interesting, however, to note that normally – and I have made this flight more times then I can count now – normally, once you leave Atlanta, you fly straight up the East Coast, staying over land or as close to land as possible for as long as possible. Then, once you get up over Nova Scotia and Gander, you end up going on the actual oceanic leg of this flight. For obvious reasons, we stayed a lot further off the coast this time. I think probably the flight plans had been in some ways modified because, if this plane, loaded with fuel obviously because it was going over seas, had made a sudden direct turn toward Philadelphia, New York or Washington as we were flying up the coast, it would have been pretty obvious to the people tracking. That was just another reminder of where we are in the world that we currently live in.

Getting to Ireland was a little tricky, but once there I was able to begin to think about what I'm going to do now with the rest of my life in a way that I might not have been able to do even two or three months ago. It's very obvious that changes need to be made, and they will either happen to you or you can make them happen. As much as possible, I'd prefer to be proactive and do what I can to formulate what I'm doing with my own life and in my own life.

That, of course, for everybody, I think, certainly for me, is easier said then done.

I was thinking as I was getting off the plane and dragging off my luggage and all the things you do and getting in the car and heading down to the house. It is 140 miles from the airport to the house in which I live in Ireland, and it is a long 140 miles. Normally, this is not something I would do all alone each time. Either I would be meeting somebody or my husband would be meeting me at the other end. But I'm on my own now, and so that's another reminder.

I have the sense of a loss, of tactile deprivation, of the loss of human contact. It isn't that I'm not seeing people or being with people or talking to people or sharing things with people, because I am. But there is, and after a while you begin to realize and really miss the fact, there is no one to hold your hand, there is no one to take your elbow as you cross the street, there is no one to put his arm around your shoulder, there is no one to cuddle with, and the longer that loss goes on, the more acutely aware of it you become.

Some of the feelings that you suppress, or at least that I probably did for the first few months, are all there and ready to show their ugly heads at some point. But the human mind is evidently geared in a very kind way because all of these things don't jump up at you and bite you quite the same way all at once.

By now I am beginning to truly miss reaching over and having a warm body next to me and somebody to sit next to in the movies, all of those kinds of things. It's not big deal stuff, it's everyday human contact things. It's even just the lack of those touchy, feely, tactile sensory experiences, it's the lack of them with the one person that I most want to share those experiences with and who I cannot bring back or will to come back. So that is another little surprise that just keeps sort of popping up at you.

I have discovered that I, at first, would have a lot of dreams about my husband. I even used to see him, I really did see him, in a sort of a semi-aware kind of state. I didn't allow myself to talk to him because that was too painful, it was too much of a reminder that there wasn't going to be anybody on the other side of this conversation, and there wasn't going to be any feed back. So when I would be going some place and seeing something I knew would be of interest to him, something as really mundane and simple as a new state highway that had opened in Houston, I would think about this. I would think that this is the one he had specifically been waiting for because it was going to cut 15 or 20 minutes off a particular trip we had to make.

And he was right. Once it was opened it absolutely did save time, and I thought to myself the first time I was on the highway and I had seen that it had opened, "Oh my God, Larry will be so excited to see that this is finally opened." Well, of course, he won't.

Now I'm at a stage where I can sort of talk to him and say, "Oh, look here, it's been opened," or "Did you see such and such had happened?" or "You'd really like this, Larry, this is really a great thing," or "This is really a shitty thing, and you really should be grateful you're not having to deal with this." So I talk to him as if he were kind of there, although I am very much aware that he is not there. I run these things by somebody who knows what's going on because I have to be sure that I am not loosing my marbles in the process of doing all of this. But it seems to be kind of a natural enough thing to talk to him. Maybe at some point I will have the feeling that he's hearing me and is talking back or at least he's listening.

We had a wonderful event that actually detained my leaving for Ireland longer then I had planned. I would have been here before my anniversary, before 911, except for the fact that one of the major organizations in Houston chose my late husband and me as its honorees of the year, which was a wonderful, lovely honor, and therefore I needed to be in Houston.

More than 500 people showed up, which was a marvelous tribute. The family was very touched, and I certainly was very touched. I joked about how we had had opportunities to be on a stage together before for different things, around a platform or at a dais, but I could honestly say that in all of those experiences in all of those years, this was the only time I got to do all of the talking. Everybody in the room who knew my husband laughed and recognized that, yes ma'am, this was true, this was probably the only time and the only circumstance in which I would get to do all of the talking.

I thought back as I was coming over on the plane, and as I was thinking about our anniversary and all of the things that one thinks about, and I got to thinking about how we had met originally and what a wonderful story that was. I wanted to be sure that not only the children but the grandchildren as well were ultimately aware of how we met.

We were introduced by a mutual friend who was a rabbi from Boston. I was living outside Detroit, and Larry was living in Houston. We were introduced at a rabbinical seminary in Cincinnati. He was there for, I think, about a three-day workshop, and I had been asked to give the Saturday evening keynote speech. Therefore, we were introduced by way of the, "Do you know so and so, have you met so and so?" kinds of introductions that people make all of the time. Little did we know that six months later we would be married.

It was a wonderful whirlwind love story. We joked about the fact that we really had to get married when we did because we no longer could afford the long distance phone bills. So, low and behold, after six months of a long distance and a whirlwind, exciting romance, mostly conducted over the telephone, we ended up married. Around the offices of this conference called The Union of American Hebrew Congregations, the joke was that we were truly the union of American Hebrew Congregations. It was a wonderful way and had all of the trappings of the things that were important to us, all of the values we cherished.

You know when you meet people under those kinds of circumstances, you're meeting someone who shares interests and values and concerns and traditions that are important to you also. That was a very lovely way for us to get to know each other. We spent many, many a long night just talking away on the telephone, getting a chance to really explore the things we each cared about, which again was a very charming way to get to know somebody. I had lots of opportunities to think about that, and what a special thing that was that we had met under those circumstances.

It wasn't somebody fixing you up, it wasn't somebody you met at a bar, it wasn't any of those kinds of things. It was just a very nice non-threatening, very sweet way for two people to meet who ended up falling very much in love and marrying and creating a life.

One of the many things we shared a great interest in was theater. We had different interests in theater. I like heavy-duty theater, I like legitimate theater, I would sit for five hours at a Eugene O'Neill play and think it was wonderful, and Larry would suffer but he would go. He liked, preferred anyway, musical theater. We went to various Broadway musicals that were fun and entertaining, and I enjoyed and I sat through them, too, because that was his preference.

We went to New York two or three times a year, and we always mapped our theater. We had so many nights or afternoons of doing musicals and so many nights of doing legitimate theater. We became members of the Irish Repertory theater and would head down to the village and catch whatever was playing at the Irish Rep., if there was something going on when we were there. We had certainly been to Carnegie Hall, we had been to Lincoln Center and we saw Wynton Marsalis do a wonderful testimonial to Oscar Peterson. That was Larry's great mentor, his jazz mentor. There were things we shared for all of our lives together.

Not so very long ago, PBS had a special, a series that ran for several nights called the Changing Stages Series, and it was a wonderful expose on the history of theater. The principal locales were in New York, London and Dublin and featuring a piece on Tennessee Williams in New Orleans. I watched it with great fascination and really had a sort of sentimental experience because we had been to theater in all of those places, and I would see the particular theater and I would say, "I remember we went there and we saw this." It was really a trip down memory lane in many ways. It was very nostalgic, particularly the part about Tennessee Williams in New Orleans because we had been to New Orleans for our honeymoon, and we had been to New Orleans again the last anniversary we had before my husband died. So that had great significance.

I honestly can say that at this point I have no desire right now to go to either New Orleans or to the theater because it would just be too painful or too lonely to be going by myself. However, I think the time will come when I can do things that we did and do them without my husband and remember and enjoy the memory without feeling the hurt and the pain of his absence in quite the same way. It's pretty raw meat right now, and I can't honestly say that I can do that.

So there are a lot of things I avoid, not because I wish to be antisocial or because I don't like a particular thing. It's because it's just too soon for me to be sitting in a darkened theater, have the lights go down and the curtain go up, and there is nobody sitting there next to me to get excited with and share that experience. Those are the kinds of things I just have to put on hold, which I think, is okay to postpone, the things we shared that were so special you don't want to do them by yourself.

It is why I wanted so desperately not to be at home for our wedding anniversary because among other things we had a tradition, a really charming lovely tradition of purchasing a fabulous glass, some wonderful piece of crystal, a unique piece of crystal each year for our anniversary. We toasted each other in that glass with champagne, and we washed it and put it in the cabinet on display, and no one else ever drank from it, and we never drank from it again. Thus, we have this wonderful collection of beautiful glass, all of them unique, all of them different, and we have indicated which one went with which year, etc. Everyday I go by that display in the dining room and see all of those glasses, and it struck me really like a bolt that there will be no more glasses, that's it.

Usually when it gets to be August or September we're starting to go shopping for our glass. This year, of course, that didn't happen and it won't ever happen again. It's such a visual reminder of the limited number of years and limited number of days that any of us is allowed. Of course, we don't know that, and we have no way of knowing that. It's probably a mercy that we have no way of knowing, but it sure is an up-front reminder to me when I go by those glasses that this is the end of the glass collection we used to observe our wedding anniversary.

I also had, perhaps one might imagine, many, many, many people who sent condolences and sympathies or made donations, which was very lovely, to causes that were special to us. Most of those came within the first month or two. After I had written something like 900 responses, I frankly lost track of how many but it was a lot. Then, five or six months after my husband died, I received a letter from a man we both knew, telling me that he had been away when my husband died and just hadn't been able to find the words the many times he'd sat down to write me this letter. One of the things that was so special about this particular letter is that he mentioned how he and Larry had had lots of discussions and that while most of them were not particularly deep or whatever, one concerned Larry's relationship with me. He wrote "Larry had spoken about what profound happiness, peace and sense of completeness and purpose he had found with you and was so thankful to you for having brought that to him."

I was so appreciative of that because, naturally enough, very few people wrote about what they knew or thought they knew or observed about my husband in relationship to me. They wrote about obviously their awareness, their experience, the stories they told about their relationship with him. Here was someone, however, who not only shared what he had experienced with Larry but what Larry had told him about our relationship together, what I had meant in his life.

That coming as it did, when it did, was such a gift, and I was so appreciative. Frankly, I was grateful that he didn't send it to me at the very beginning because I probably wouldn't have appreciated it when I was going through so many pieces of mail. But it was lovely to get it and his timing actually was very excellent.

Heartbeats:

• Get good medical attention, your body has taken a real beating, know what is normal for a grieving person.

• Because you loved much, you hurt deeply, but think what you would have missed other wise.

• Focus on the joy this person brought to you, let that be their legacy not the final pain.

• Never let the only link to your loved one be the pain that will become its own unhealthy payoff.

• Because he loved me he would not want me to hurt for-ever.

Listen and Learn

CHAPTER 9

*O*ne of the great learning experiences for me in the past six months has been to revisit my appreciation for the company, the counsel and the comfort of women. I was, at the behest of my parents, educated in girl schools all the way through and up to and including undergraduate school. One of the multiple gifts that education provided me was the fact that I learned to cooperate with, work with and value the opinions of other women. In my subsequent adult life, at one point, I served as the executive director for a not-for-profit agency. All the people who were employed were women, and women liked working for me. They would tell me that, and they would also apply for a job saying, "We heard that working with you is really a good working environment."

I think I probably learned a great deal about all of this because I was surrounded in my formative years by women, girls and certainly older women. The experiences that women are now sharing with me are experiences that are similar to those I am undergoing. As an example, I have a friend who was a widow for 11 years. She asked me if, after the September 11th crash and the subsequent financial fall out, was I afraid, did that frighten me?

I said, "Yes it did."

She said, "Good, it should frighten you. For the first year, everything should frighten you because you're still getting your bearings. And even though you'll have lots of reassurance, and it's probably correct that all is going to be well, you're very new at this game of managing your life and your finances solely on your own, and your responsibilities and your properties, etc. Therefore, it's fine, it's a good thing that you should be afraid."

It was very reassuring to me that she had been there and done that. She had told me what it was like for her, gradually crawling out of the experience of being alone and forming a new life. She was widowed at a much younger age and subsequently she did remarry. She was widowed for 11 years, and 11 years gives you a lot of learning experience. This is the sort of thing that has been so lovely since most people who offer unsolicited advice, and are very quick to offer it, are people who usually have not walked the walk. They are very big on talking the talk but they've not walked the walk.

My caution to anybody in my own experience is, listen to the people who've been there and done that. If you are a woman, listen to the women who have been through what you are going through and who at the appropriate times will offer to share an experience or feeling or a piece of advice and counsel. Those are the people whose wisdom has been of great comfort to me. I think about how brave a lot of these women have been because some of them were left young, some of them were left with dependant children. I was not, and that certainly makes my life infinitely easier.

I visited with a woman who was telling me that she had had a stressful day because her second eldest child had just decided that, after an illustrious career of three weeks in college, he didn't like it and thought he should leave. She was obviously stressed over this. They'd paid his tuition, had gotten an apartment and now after three weeks he was quitting.

In the midst of this conversation about kids and the decisions they make and how difficult it can be and so on, she came to tell me how two years earlier her mother, in her mid-to-late 70's, had had a stroke and thought her days were numbered. On top of this, she had had a heart attack and some other problems. Well, she has recovered to the point were she is basically physically alive but needs a feeding tube. She's like a baby but unlike an infant who will grow into more self reliance, this is her mother who is infantile and will always be for as long as she lives, and no one can say how long at this point that will be.

So she and her sister, who are now at the stage of their lives when one would hope to be doing other things, are now taking over the care, the feeding, the clothing, the bathing, and the all that is required of their mother. Not complaining about it but it has now become another aspect of their lives. The rest of her life still goes on, the rest of her family the rest of her obligations, etc. I don't observe men doing this in the same capacity so, therefore, I'm looking to and being encouraged by the experiences of women. She's not complaining, she's just telling me, this is now where they are and what they have to do. She knows they have to get on with it.

I'm going to indulge in a small bit of sexist trivia now. When I'm in Ireland and look out the front of this house, I look toward the ocean and see a meadow between myself and the ocean. In that meadow graze maybe a dozen cows and one bull. One day I noticed it was very, very windy and very rainy. I found out later the winds were something like 50 to 60 m.p.h. All of the cows and all of the babies went over to the hedges and stood with their faces in the hedge as a shelter from the rain. The mothers gathered up the small ones, and they all walked over and did that. The bull on the other hand stood in the middle of this field and toughed it out.

Whether he was doing a macho thing, whether he didn't know the difference, whether he didn't want to be in the company of the females and the babies, I don't know. But it was so funny to see the females gathering up and nurturing the small ones to get them into shelter while the male just stood there till the storm blew over and the rain had stopped. I thought it was an interesting observation, and I'm wondering if there is something in the species, something in the human and animal kingdom whereby women end up doing things for themselves and for their families, that we have become soft-wired to preserve ourselves and our kids and in many cases our parent generation.

It's something certainly I'm becoming increasingly aware of as those of us in the sandwich generation who have new dependant children, for many women in my situation still have kids who are not married or who are not self sufficient and then aging parents. All of that can be a very long and difficult time for anybody and certainly, if in the midst of all of that, you're left on your own, I'm sure it is even increasingly more difficult.

I have a friend, Joe Slade, who is an accomplished poet and artist and best of all a wonderful human being and a wonderful friend. In one of her pieces of poetry, a poem called, *A Recollection of a Dream*, she has a couple of lines I think about over and over again.

"To love you, I must find the cave of your disappointment."

I have thought about that so often in relation to how I am sorting out the feelings, the complications of my feelings, about my husband and my marriage and the moving on in my life and the letting go of things, letting go of him, and letting go of things good, bad and otherwise that are now just part of the fiber of my being.

My husband had a true creative genius. As a kid he could sing, and he could dance, and he learned to play the piano. He used all of those talents in his business. When he would create an ad campaign, it was Katy bar the door. He hit the floor running. He had wonderful ideas, he energized the place, he could be presented reams of material and really in a very short time come up with something that was so clever and so right-on and so memorable that often times, it seemed to me, it would take awhile for the client to appreciate. He could do this so quickly, the value of what it was he had done took awhile to recognize, to understand.

It's probably true that anybody who is that creative is a very complicated human being. In exploring the nature of my husband and therefore the nature of us, I'm trying to be honest, and I'm trying to be honorable, and I'm trying to be respectful of his memory. He was funny, he was fun, he was erasable, he could be irritable, he was challenging, he was a creature of impulse, and he was a person who because of his own unique childhood experiences felt a very strong obligation to carry the weight of, if not the world, a sizable portion of it on his own shoulders. He therefore was a wonderful friend, a great mentor, a wonderful advisor.

People in droves came to him, people loved him and nobody more than I. That was in many ways a need of his for validation, he had a tremendous need for affirmation. Living with someone who is that needy is sometimes really difficult. It is also, I suspect, part of why, when he realized that he had made some judgment calls in terms of juggling finances that were very dicey and not in his own best interest, he really began to become extraordinarily stressed. What he wouldn't do, probably because he couldn't, was share with anybody, anybody who could have helped him in any capacity, the dilemma he felt he was facing.

As he was working longer and harder and being more obviously stressed, his health was, to me, not what it should have been. I was saying to him, why don't you just take a day off, why don't you go play golf, why don't you go to bed early while we're in Ireland, why don't you turn the computer off and not bring your work with you. One of the mixed blessings of the computer age is that you never go any place without taking your work with you. So between the cell phone and the computer, it didn't matter where he went, the work and the office and the stock market and all of that went with him.

I would say, "What is the good of having this great place to go and relax if you go there and you can't really spend the time relaxing." That was a very sensible, logical thing to say but, in retrospect, I'm sure all I was doing was adding to his stress level because he couldn't say to me, for his own reasons, "I can't. I just can't do that. I've got a situation here that I can't just let go. I'm so concerned, I'm so worried about it I just can't let it go."

I would ask him, "Well, do you not have competent people?"

He would say, "Yes, I do but they are not rainmakers, and they can't do what I do."

That was true, they couldn't, they can't. His inability to share with me, with his attorney, with his son who really is in a business where he could have assisted him with some of this financial management situation, simply was something he could not do. His pride, his sense of his own need to manage everything simply would not permit that. When you're raised as he was, in a family where so many people's sense of achievement or pride is placed on this one kid, and you have internalized that, it's very difficult for that kid to turn around and say, "I can't do this, I've made a judgment error here, and I need to have somebody walk me through it." It would have meant for us, I think, prudent and significant changes in lifestyle, which I was really prepared to make.

One of the things Larry would say to me and to other folks is why he would do something i.e., I was in Ireland, and he decided on his own to buy me a more expensive car. I was fine with the one I had, but he felt it was more important that I should have this other car.

I would say, "It's lovely but why?"

He would say, because you never asked for anything extravagant or exorbitant or whatever, and therefore he did these things because he wanted to and out of love. He did wonderfully, lovely things that I will always treasure.

This downsizing of lifestyle would have been very difficult for him because he finally had reached a point where he felt he had his eye on the prize. He really felt that he was almost home free to a point where he'd never have to worry again. It was an interesting thing, as he would say, that no one can touch us anymore, no one can take anything away from us. I never understood who he thought was going to try to take anything away from him, but he did at some level. He died before the worst of the sorting out, which did get sorted out, it was doable. Many a night I have laid awake and wondered if part of his own neglect of his health and his own inability, even for a short time, to get off the treadmill he was on was the realization that it would be better for him to go out in a blaze of glory than it would be for him to have to face some of the difficult stuff that eventually, probably everybody in business in America, ends up facing.

What he was facing in March, tons of people were facing by September, and most would one way or another make it through. If the business didn't make it, then they'd pack it in and go on and do something else. In my husband's case, he <u>was</u> his business. It was his alter ego, it was the thing he loved most in the world, more then me, more then the children, more then anything. It <u>was</u> Larry.

The thought that something might have happened that could have jeopardized his business and his ability to live the life he desired and had finally acquired was probably more than he would have been prepared for. He worked so long and so hard for this he would not have been prepared for a down turn. It was a sad thing to think that so many of the things he worked a lifetime for he never lived to enjoy. The judgment calls he made financially in the market, for instance, would have been risky for somebody in their 40's, they were unbelievable for somebody in their 60's.

Certainly there is no way of ever knowing this for sure or verifying this, but I will always believe, based on the autopsy report, that because of the severe arterial damage and because of the numbers of small strokes, mini-strokes he had, that this physical condition had affected his judgment. I think he was making judgment calls he might not have made under other circumstances. While I have no way of certainly proving that, it seems to fit a certain kind of a pattern, a certain kind of logic. That a person who had worked so long and so hard to acquire what he had was now taking such risk with it seemed in a sense out of character. I understand right along with anybody who gambled with him that he basically gambled kind of the same way. He didn't pick up his chips and take his toys and go home when he had won; he would hang out until he had lost it all and then hope for the best the next time the wheel rolled around.

It has occurred to me that he may have been a person, obviously this is a speculation on my part, who suffered from what I think is called the "imposter syndrome," where people become very successful and somehow, at some level, don't really believe they are entitled to the success. I think the drill goes something like this: if people really knew what I was like they wouldn't think this much of me, or whatever. It's a fairly common phenomenon, and the only reason I tend to think there may be some in his case is that on more than one occasion he mentioned to me that he thought there was a possibility he could be experiencing some of these same kinds of feelings. The same kind of feelings so prevalent in people who exhibit this imposter syndrome.

All of these were things that would lead to upping the ante with a person's stress level. A lot of his stresses were self-imposed because he had the kind of mind that was mercurial, it would jump from this and that and the other, and he made these wonderful out-of-the-box connections and ideas. You would think, "Where does this come from?"

That's the upside of that sort of a mind. The downside of that sort of a mind is that staying focused is really a challenge, to get him to stay focused on something and to stay task- oriented was really, really difficult. Therefore, the use of his time-management skills was not what you would call outstanding. His sense of time was null and void, and his time management was not that great, so he ended up imposing stresses on himself that probably he could have avoided had he had a better handle on how to stay task-oriented and focused.

However, had he been able to do all of those things, maybe he would have been an accountant instead of a creative wizard. So there is a tradeoff for all of us in everything.

I think back about the last couple of years of his life in particular and realize that he had enough discomfort that he had finally gone to a cardiologist. He had had the angiogram, and he had the angioplasty, and he was suppose to do certain lifestyle changes in terms of what he ate, what he didn't eat, exercise, weight reduction, none of which he did. He went to the cardiac rehab once and told me he didn't like that, and that was it.

He had had a wake up call, a TIA (temporary ischaemic attack), mini-stroke, many years ago and was told then that he had a lot of cholesterol in his carotid artery and really needed to watch what he ate. He also needed to do the exercising and quit smoking. He did quit smoking but the other things he just kind of ignored and pushed himself at a very hard pace. Other people who either worked with him or knew him in other capacities have since said to me that Larry seemed different in the past year or two. I think that he probably was different, that he was not feeling well a whole bunch of the time. He was in major duty denial because he didn't want to face the fact that maybe he had a serious health problem. He could see that a lot of the financial things he had thought were going to be home runs were looking more like foul balls, and the economy was headed south and he with it.

All of these things were major stress producers, choosing to spin as much as you can, to move stuff from here to there and keep all the plates spinning. The biggest spin of all is to keep everybody laughing all the time while you're doing all of this and this takes an incredible toll. I think in many ways he just wore out, his heart wore out, his system, his mind just gave out. Of course, the loss to me, when we had all of these wonderful plans of what we were going to do in our retirement years, which were presumably only a few years away, was terrible.

Maybe retirement would have been such a nightmare for him that stress in itself would have caused him to have a heart attack, I don't know. But he never got the chance to really try it. He thought he could do some consulting in Ireland, he could write a book there, he could have done all of the above and it would have been fun for him to have the opportunity to have the economic freedom to just do what he wanted to do. However, when I would talk to him about scaling back or maybe we didn't need to do every obligatory community social event, etc., etc., his response to me was, "Either you're a player or you're not a player."

Once you give up these things, you're not up-front and center, you're no longer a player. I don't have the frame of reference for a business in the same way as he to know whether that's true or false. It probably is, and it certainly was for him. If he didn't walk into a restaurant and have people know who he was, he was not happy. He didn't like to try new places all that much because he would have to start all over again getting to know the chef and the maître d' and the owner and all of that sort of thing.

Larry liked to be acknowledged and to be the center of attention. He truly had a real need to be the center of attention a lot of the time. I know that was hard for me on many occasions. Someone once said to me after Larry died, "I had dinner with another woman friend some months ago and saw the two of you come in to a local deli for lunch, and Larry immediately went to a table were he knew people to start telling jokes." She said, "It must have been very hard for you when you couldn't really just sit down and have a conversation because there was always a story to be told, a joke to be told and somebody to talk to." I said, "Yeah! There were times when it really was."

It was certainly the charm of my husband, it was what made him the bon vivant that he was, and it was enervating to me. On the Meyer Briggs scale of personality traits, it was helpful for me to understand that this was a division of personality that was certainly operative in our life. One is, the personality who at the end of a work day is tired and gets the juices flowing again by going to a party, going out to dinner, being with a lot of people, lots of talk, lots of activity, etc. That was Larry.

There are other people who at the end of a day, when they're tired and they've been up and on all day long with people, need down time. They need to be by themselves, they need some quite time, they need to be with maybe one or two people, they don't need a whole crowd of people. Instead of charging their batteries, it drains their batteries. That's me. Obviously, we had a lot of accommodating to do and eventually did, over the course of years, learn how to do it.

When I would begin to look and say, "Do we always need to be the last people to leave?" He'd say, "No, you're right, we can go now." But his batteries were charged by constantly being around a lot of people. It was all superficial stuff, it was light fluffy small talk, and it's what people do.

It's what you do when you are at a social engagement. You don't go out to have a social evening with people so you can discuss Nietzsche and Kant, you don't do that kind of thing, that's not what social small talk is all about. Larry was an expert at that, he was very able to discuss deeper and more substantial things and often times, when we would be taking a trip in the car, we'd be talking about philosophy, history or politics. But in a room with a bunch of folks, my husband was the person who was often times the center of attention and needed to do that. I'm sure knowing, not a whole lot, but knowing what I know about what makes people tick and where this stuff comes from, this was something from his childhood, he was a child performer.

I have a strong feeling that my husband's sense of who he was and his value in the world had to do with his performance. I don't mean like tap dancing and that sort of thing, although as a kid that was a big deal to him, too. As an adult it was a question of his performance, which led to one of the more telling and salient moments in a discussion we had. We didn't know each other as teenagers so we were talking about our teenage years and our growing up, etc.

He asked, "Did you really ever fail at something, did you really ever blow it or do something that was embarrassing, loose an election or fail a class?"

I said, "Sure everybody has stuff."

I told him I had a terrible time with geometry, and my father made me go to summer school to raise my grade. I didn't fail it but I got a C. That just wasn't good enough for my dad, so I had to go to summer school and raise my grade. I had to go to summer school in a public school and, of course, I'd been in these girls schools in this sequestered environment so I felt I was being, on top of geometry, subjected to a "blackboard jungle." All of which was a great exaggeration. It was just that my limited experience with public, inner-city high schools was between zero and nothing.

I said if I failed at something, or something didn't go well, or I was having a bad time with a teacher at school or something, I was always anxious to get home. Larry looked at me as though I had just spoken to him in a foreign tongue. He said, "to go home?" I said, "Of course." To go home was the place where things were all right. So you didn't do well, so you'd take it again and you'd do better, or you lost this election so you'd run for something else and you'd do better the next time.

Obviously, that was not an experience he would have had. I think that was a very telling thing about his sense of who he was. He presented a fabulously secure or brave façade, and much of it was genuine. There were a lot of things that gnawed at him that I think made life hard for him. I think those are things that probably go way, way back, things that I struggled with because we came from different environments.

I tended to be more logical, more analytical. We were really like a gender flip, and that would annoy him because he wanted me to be more free flowing in things. In retrospect it was a good balance because here were two people whose personalities complemented one another and sometimes came into collision with one another. We supplied what the other person needed. I probably supplied him with a sense of balance and a sense of ballast and, according to the friend I mentioned in the letter, a purpose and a peace and a calmness in his life, and I'm so grateful for that.

He on the other hand supplied me with a living experience of the Stephen Sondheim song about how anyone can whistle. Cleo Lane sings it beautifully. Anyone can whistle any old time, but it isn't easy for her. What's easy for her is translating Greek and climbing a mountain. All of those things were easy but to be just a free spirit was not easy. That epitomized the sort of thing Larry did for me. He was my free spirit, my ability to soar, my dreamer of dreams, my seer of visions, and that was certainly a wonderful, complementary part to my personality because I don't have those flights of fancy in the same way he did. I miss it, I miss all of those things terribly because I am now trying to re-dream the dream and reformulate my visions, and I'm doing it with out the dreamer, the wizard to run them by me.

When I decided to go back to school to get my master's degree and was in my mid-to-late 40's, frankly I would have been not only happy but thrilled out of my mind to have gotten through with this master's degree. It was a masters in philosophy, and it was so hard. I would have been so happy to have just finished and said grace over being finished. Particularly since in my department I was the only person they had graduated in two years so I was real happy to be finished.

In typical Larry fashion we went to dinner and he said, "You have to make me a promise when you start this grad school thing."

I said, "yes."

He said, "You will have to promise me you'll finish."

I said, "Sure, barring natural disaster or illness, sure I'll finish."

He said, "No, you have to go all the way to a doctorate."

I said, "Come on."

He said, "No, no you can do it, you've got to do it, you'll be the first and only doctor in our family, you can do it", and I did. I know I did it certainly because I wanted to do it but I did it because in so many ways he was there encouraging me and saying to anybody who would listen, anyone he could buttonhole, how proud he was of what I was doing. He was truly all of that.

But now, my number one supporter in the world, my great cheer-er is gone, and no one else will do those things. Certainly no one will ever do them in the way he did them. I certainly miss that, I miss all of those things about him. I miss the complications of his personality, I miss the complexities, and I miss the fact that life with him was never dull and never boring. I even miss the conflict of, let's do this, no, let's do that. I miss all of that. I miss the fact that of the two of us, he was the shopper, he loved to shop. We would go to New York, and we'd split for the day, and I would go to the museum, and he'd buy clothes. Go figure, but that's the way it worked.

I miss the fact that lots of times he would come by and he would have purchased something for me and it was perfect, it looked perfect, it fit perfectly, and it was exactly the right style, color and whatever. I don't miss him because I miss the items per se, but I miss the fact that there was somebody who could do that and would do that. I don't have any desire to go, which under the circumstances is probably preciously wonderful, I have no particular desire to go and shop because I have no particular desire to dress up. Where am I going and for whom am I dressing?

I have plenty of things that are wonderful and appropriate that I can wear for a long, long time. But the idea that I would go and get an outfit for a special event we would be going to because I would so want him to be proud of the way I looked, no, I have no interest or desire to do that. There were lots of things that were not earth shattering, life-altering events but they are there, and they're just so over-arching in so many areas of life. It has been a matter of personal pride for me that I keep myself up, get my hair done, get my nails done, put my lipstick on and all that good stuff because he did take such pride in the fact that I looked presentable and looked attractive. I would not in any way wish to dishonor my husband's memory by going to seed all of a sudden and looking pretty awful. Image was crucial to Larry.

There is not much incentive to do it even though I know it's good for my mental health, and that's another point. It has made my kids proud of me to say, "We're really pleased to see that you look good mom and are keeping yourself up." It is an important indicator that you are still amongst the living. It certainly isn't the same as getting all fancied up because we're going to something wonderful or elegant, and this person you're with who really cares about you is going to be so pleased to escort you and have you look a certain way. No, that just doesn't happen.

These are the day-to-day realizations that begin to let you know your life has changed irrevocably. Many of these small, presumably insignificant things –and there are many – are feeding into me psychologically a greater understanding or an unearthing of or an opening up of some of the more complex aspects of my husband's personality, my own personality, and the warp and woof of our own relationship. It's sad that these sorts of things should come post-mortem. Everybody really who's married should be thinking about it, while you're alive and you have the person there to speak with and run the ideas by. Be that as it may, it definitely is something that happens, or at least it is happening to me. I am very fortunate that I can be open and honest with a handful of wonderful women who have had similar experiences and are good listeners and good advisors.

At one point in my life before my husband and I got married, I was in the process of getting divorced from my first husband. A friend of mine who was single at that time, I think for 10 years, and who was very sort of proper and dignified said, "I am offering you two pieces of advice." Both of which were very good by the way. One was, "Do not indulge in self-pity. It ill-becomes you." The second, which is a fabulous line: "Beware of men for whom the word lunch is a verb."

That was a fabulously funny and probably fairly true piece of information. I think about that often, and I think that certainly to indulge in self-pity does ill-become anybody. It's having a few folks you can really rely on help keep you on the straight and narrow.

John Adams is reputed to have said at one point after the French Revolution and the precarious situation in America,

"The whole drama of the world is such tragedy that I'm weary of the spectacle."

Amongst other things, I think he was a voracious writer of letters to anyone who, I guess, would listen to him, but most particularly, to his wife, Abigail, whom he always referred to as his dearest and best friend.

I think about how prescient that was said over 200 years ago. When one looks at what happened on the 11th of September and realize the world will never be the same for any of us, it's been a long time coming, and we've certainly turned a blind eye to this. But be that as it may, it will never be the same. That's on a global macroeconomic, if you will, issue. On the micro level, I realize that in my own life the tragedy, the drama of my own life is such a tragedy that it will never be the same.

The balancing act of realizing and acknowledging what is real and what is surreal, is to keep that in some sort of perspective. To be aware that to fall into pity, and most appropriately self-pity, is a form of self-indulgence that not only doesn't become, it's a luxury I truly feel I cannot afford.

Again, coming back to the wonderful counsel and comfort and company of women who can say, "Enough already, we've heard it," because there are times when you need somebody to say to you, "Just get on with it." There are times when that is appropriate, there are times when you just need somebody to sit and hold your hand and let you cry. There are times when you just need people to share their own stories with you, their own history, not telling you, "Oh, you think you have it bad? Wait till you hear what happened to me."

None of that stuff, just sharing, when I was at this stage, this is what it was like and this is what helped me. It may help you, it may not help you. But those are the kinds of things the people who have been able to put their sense of judgment in abeyance and just been there to listen, to laugh, to cry, to help, to invite you to lunch, whatever. We're going to a movie, it's a rainy day, if you're home why don't you come with us. Those are the kinds of things that are incalculably invaluable.

There is no way you can put a worth on that. These are very common things, and we often may undervalue them. In the scope of things, those are the things that have proven to be so incredibly helpful and incredibly valuable.

The letters that people wrote? I never thought it was that important before. I would write them because it was appropriate, I just didn't realize how important it was to write condolence letters. Now that I've been a recipient of condolence letters, it's an amazing comfort to have those letters, and there are literally piles and piles and piles of them from all over the world. I can go back and reread and revisit some of those at certain times. Some of them were particularly touching.

Some of them were from people who knew my husband before I did, childhood friends. They can share insights and experiences that I have no way of being privy to. Again, those are wonderful gifts. The only cost is the price of a stamp. Unless you have received them or been in a position to need to receive them, one probably doesn't have the full appreciation of how valuable they are. On my list of to-do things or to be very aware to do in the future, is to be sure that I don't let an opportunity ever go by when someone dear has been lost to write that family a condolence letter. I mean this even if it's someone I don't know particularly well because I wouldn't forget if it were someone I knew very well.

I know how important those letters are. They are a link between the person you have lost and the web of the living, whose lives they have touched. In some way, it connects you with the rest of the world, even if it is for a few short lines or a few short moments. It's an important connection. I will always remember now how much it meant to me and be sure to be extra careful to do that in the future for someone else.

Heartbeats:

- Listen to those who have been there, done that.
- Look outside yourself at how others are coping.
- Realize your limitations, you can't control another's choices no matter how much you love them or they you.
- There is always a tradeoff for everything, good or bad.
- Be aware of feeling tactile deprivation; getting a massage, a hairdo or a manicure are socially acceptable ways for human contact. Hold a baby or hold a child.
- Avoid self pity, its corrosive.
- Remember what helped you and offer the same to someone else, you'll both benefit.

Days of Awe

CHAPTER 10

*I*n the Jewish tradition, each year we celebrate what we refer to as the High Holidays. This encompasses Rosh Hashanah and Yom Kippur as well as various other holidays or observances that fall within that period of time.

It encompasses the better part of a month all together. We think of them as the Days of Awe because it is the time when we reflect on our lives, on our actions, on our relationships with God and with one another. It is a time when we take stock and do penance, and we make a commitment to do better and to go forward. Included in this are many things that are symbolic, and certainly one of the things that is very important is the remembrance at the conclusion of Yom Kippur, of all who have died and gone before us, particularly those who have died within the past year.

Rosh Hashanah means the birthday of the world or the creation of the world, and it is the time when we recognize the magnificence of God and of God's wonderful power. We recognize our commitment to God, our relationship to God, our relationship to the world and our renewal of the world. We believe that it is our responsibility to renew the world. Also, it is the time when we are what is known in the tradition as inscribed in the Book of Life.

On the first evening of Rosh Hashanah we exchange a greeting or a blessing that says in English,

"May you be inscribed and sealed for a good year, may you be written in the Book of Life."

The Book of Life is sealed for that year, traditionally 10 days following Yom Kippur. Obviously, most of us have no way of knowing which of these years will be the year in which we will not be sealed in the Book of Life. For the people left behind grieving, that is a real jolt, a real awakening. There is an observance at the end of Yom Kippur called Yizkor, which is a memorial service. It is a memorial service for which candles are lit to remember those who have preceded us in death. There is a blessing that is particularly comforting, I think, not only to people in the Jewish tradition but for anyone who is remembering someone they have lost and loved.

"We remember with sorrow those whom death has taken from our midst during the past year. Taking these dear ones into our hearts with all our beloved, we recall them now with reverence. In the rising of the sun and its going down, we remember them. In the blowing of the wind and in the chill of winter, we remember them. In the opening buds and in the rebirth of spring, we remember them. In the blueness of the sky and the warmth of summer, we remember them. In the rustling of leaves and the beauty of autumn, we remember them. In the beginning of the year and when it ends, we remember them. When we are weary and in need of strength, we remember them. When we are lost and sick at heart, we remember them. When we have joys and yearn to share, we remember them. So long as we live they too shall live for they now are a part of us as we remember them."

This has been a wonderful source of comfort to me, certainly to many other people as well. The realization that in some way the remembrance of, and the carrying forth of the memory of the loved one that we have lost, is a way of keeping their presence alive in the world and alive with us. There is another lovely blessing that goes:

"To celebrate life is to acknowledge the ongoing dying and ultimately to embrace death. For although all life travels towards its death, death is not a destination, it is a journey to beginnings. All death leads to life again. From peelings to mulch to new potatoes the world is ever renewing, ever renewed."

As I just mentioned, there are many symbolic traditions that accompany the Days of Awe experience and that time. One of them is a little known symbol, ceremony really, called Tashlich. This is done on the afternoon of the first day of Rosh Hashanah. What one tends to do is go to a body of flowing water, and you have bread crumbs in your pocket, and you throw your bread crumbs onto the water, and the bread crumbs are absorbed and swept away and disappear. Those are representative of your sins of the past year, that you are eliminating yourself of those sins, you are freeing yourself from them. You are letting them go with the expectation that you will not reclaim them in some way by redoing what you have done in the past, in the coming year.

It's a wonderful symbolism and it's a great thing to do with children because it makes an abstract idea for them very much more concrete. It also has been something that I have amended and made to work for me as a person who's working my way through this experience of being widowed. I decided not to write down all of the sins I had committed, God knows there are enough of those to go around, but to take the offenses I had experienced – the slights, the injuries, the grudges, etc., etc. – write them and the names of the people involved on little pieces of paper, take the pieces of paper down to the ocean while I was in my home in Ireland, rip them up and scatter them and give them a burial at sea.

What I have discovered is that there are three little words that are most important to the human experience. No they are not, "I Love You." The three little words are, "Let It Go." It is so easy to harbor the things and clutch to one's bosom, the things that have bothered you. I don't know if this is true of everyone but it certainly is true of me. In the course of my lifetime, I have conveniently let slide or omitted or just not remembered the multitude of kindnesses and gracious acts and good deeds and courtesies and all of those things that people have done for me. I remember, however, with total recall, date, time and place, all of the slights, all of the insults, all of the hurts, all of the whatever's that happened to me. I can tell you to the day who said what to me, be it 15 years ago or 15 minutes ago. To carry that psychic weight is a very heavy and stressful burden, and there is no payoff, there is absolutely no payoff.

What I have done is I have made a list of all of those things I can think of that I have been harboring in my little heart and my little cache of deeds that have not been done that were good to me, and I have destroyed them. I have written them, I have scattered them, and I have let them go. It is in a sense as though I have been liberated from a burden that I had no need to carry and certainly have no need or, frankly, the energy to carry in the future.

One of the things you become so acutely aware of when you face death as we did with the loss of my husband is the precariousness of life, the very tenuousness of life, and you never know, you just never know, when you are going to be called, and you don't know how many days you have on this earth. To waste the days one has or the energy one has harboring negative thoughts that aren't going to get you anything is just not productive.

My husband used to always ask, and it was really very wise, when he or I or anybody was stewing over something, "What are we getting out of this?" The answer often times was, "Not a damn thing!" There is nothing one gets other than perhaps elevated blood pressure and increased grief and aggravation out of harboring the grudges that some of us have nurtured for the better part of a life-time. Letting them go and watching them literally float out to sea was a very liberating experience.

There are some things, unfortunately, that will not let go of me; the grief, the loneliness, the emptiness, I can't just will those or toss those away. Those things that I can control, I will. Each time in my life I can be proactive in something rather then just reactive, I'm strengthened and I strengthen my will to go forward.

One lovely fall evening in Ireland I attended a Russian string quartet concert held at Bantry House, a manor house over 200 years old. The concert was sonorous Russian music, which was dedicated to those who had died on September 11th. The room was an elegant old library with two massive fireplaces on either end and in the center of which was a magnificent chandelier that was actually lit by candles.

Larry would have loved this. He truly enjoyed all kinds of music and especially chamber music. He was himself of Russian background. I was with wonderful friends, and I met new ones, all of which he would very much have loved. As I set there I thought, "This one's for you, dear. I'll live my life for two people as best I can."

It's a way in which I can feel his presence in situations where I know he would have derived great pleasure. It's a reminder of the prayer that we have said at the end of Yom Kippur about finding a person, remembering the presence, being in the rustling of the leaves and in the setting of the sun and in the mountains. His presence will always be for me in anything that is musical. His spirit will be alive as long as I can keep that memory and as long as I can share in the things that the two of us enjoyed so much together. I really am in many ways living for two people.

I don't know if that is realistic, I don't know if that's even a healthy thing to do. But I feel as though I'm living the life that has been granted to me, and I'm living for him, doing the things he would have felt were so important – maintaining the home in Ireland, maintaining certain things that he valued so much, those are the things I would do for him.

There is another prayer, a childhood prayer that is probably known to everyone. One of the first things many people teach their kids is the prayer that goes:

"Now I lay me down to sleep, I pray the Lord my soul to keep, if I should die before I wake, I pray the Lord my soul to take." The line that jumps out at me is, "If I should die before I wake."

Wouldn't that be lovely? Wouldn't that be the easiest way to just slip into the next world? To just go to sleep and not wake up.

It's probably how everyone would hope to die rather then to be ill or to be in an accident or incapacitated, to just simply go to sleep and not waken. That to me is the easy part. At this point, dying would be the easy part, living is the hard part. Yet, each time I pick myself up and dust myself off and do something that is productive or is even enjoyable because it's okay since you're alive to enjoy your life. There is no walking around in widow's weeds and wringing your hands and carrying on forever, this is no testament of any value to the person who has died. They have not only lost their life, you are now surrendering yours, and life is too precious a gift. We can't give it, we can only appreciate and use it. If I could have given it, I would have. As I said to my husband as he lay in his hospital bed in intensive care, "If I could do this for you, I would do this for you," and I would have but I couldn't. I can't give life to anyone.

Yes, of course, one gives birth, and in that sense one gives life but one doesn't really give life to anyone. To not appreciate the value of life for as long as it is given you is such an insult to the God to whom you pray and who has endowed you with life. It also is an insult to the people who have already gone before you and left you with the legacy of their love and their commitments and their vitality. It does them no good for you to squander those resources, and it does you no good as the survivor to squander those resources. I try to go forward with an appreciation of the things I see around me and to strip away the things that are physically negative or tiresome or counter productive.

I do not ascribe to the theory of the age of Enlightenment that human beings are perfectible. I think we sort of lurch along, we are one step forward and two steps backward. We all are the walking wounded so we do the best we can. Even at that, to not acknowledge what a wonderful gift being alive is, painful as it is, is an insult to us, the God who gives us life, and it insults really those for whom their life has been removed. That is a message, a thought, an inspiration that keeps me going on many, many days when it would be easier to pull the covers over my head and just say, "The hell with it, I'm not getting up, I'm not going forward, I'm not going to do anything,"

Once the burdensome part of being widowed has passed, and along with it the intensive level of activity, and everyone who knows you has begun to accept the fact that, yes, you are one and not two now, that life has irrevocably changed and you have begun to settle in to a routine, some of it just plain dull and dreary, it would be, I think, easier to give up six months down the road than it is at the very beginning. I'm no longer numb, I'm no longer in denial, I don't have as much anger fueling me and getting me up and getting me going, although the anger does serve a purpose. It is now a question of how to deal with the sadness, the emptiness and the inclination to despair.

Looking at the beauties of life, looking at a child, a new baby, looking at a gorgeous sunset, looking at the marvel of anything living, looking at the small things such as picking the blackberries in my own field, are the things that keep me appreciative of the power of life and the need to rejoice in life. These are things that are very encouraging and strengthening. Rejoicing seems like a very strange term to be using but it is, I think, appropriate to say, I had X number of years that were better than most people who might have had twice as many years, and I rejoice in that memory.

Do I wish it were more? Definitely. Do I grieve at the loss? Constantly. Do I think about it all the time, every waking moment? Does it effect every decision I make? Absolutely. However, what would my life have been like had we not had this experience, had we not had this relationship. I would have missed so much.

I would have been spared this pain, absolutely, but I would have also been spared the love and the excitement and the tumult and the interesting things and the challenging things and the innovative things and the creative things, and all of those experiences, I would have missed those also. Those would have been far too wonderful to have passed on in order to have been spared the pain of this loss.

At some point in my life, at the end, I hope we will be reunited and I will have all kinds of things to tell him about, such things as, "This is what I did and this is how it worked out." He would be there and say, "I know, I was watching and you did okay, you did fine." This is something I think about a lot, about when the time comes for me to be reunited with my husband.

My mother-in-law of blessed memory truly, truly believed she was going to be reunited with her parents when she died. She died a very difficult death, a lingering death of cancer and a very painful death. What sustained her and got her through it was the belief that when she died she was going to be reunited with her mother and her father. Who are we to say, by the way, that she is not. That was a great sustaining strength to her.

I have copied a lesson from her Life Book and have decided that I too will look forward to being together again. Until the moment of truth, no one knows whether this will actually happen or not but it helps. Anything that helps get you from one day to the next, unless it's terribly destructive and counter productive, is a good thing. Getting up, getting dressed, putting on your shoes, going out, doing what you have to do takes an awful lot of effort, and it's part of the reason why denuding myself of negative psychological baggage I don't need to carry, has become a very energizing and liberating experience.

I, frankly, don't have the energy any longer to carry around things that are not going to be useful. If somebody did something to me 20 years ago that I didn't like, so what! It's over, it's finished, it can't be redone, it can't be undone, it's water under the bridge, it doesn't matter. "Let it go" has become my new mantra and has certainly been an example of the most important three little words I've experienced in my recent lifetime.

Yes, it is wonderful to hear, "I love you," especially from the person that you most need to hear it from; that is a very important thing to hear. Once you have heard that, and once you know that and you are secure in that, there are other things in other parts of your business that you need to care for. Certainly to let it go is a critical life message. I would love to be able to give that insight, open up my kids' heads and say, "Get over it, let it go, move on." You can't do that for anybody. Nobody could have done it for me, and it took me this long, perhaps I'm a slow learner, but it took me this long to get there. Once having gotten there, it made my life so much simpler and so much easier, perhaps because I have so many things that are real to cope with. Not baby stuff, not nonsense stuff, not petty stuff, real difficult stuff that one learns to triage emotionally and to prioritize.

It would have been a great lesson had I been able to learn it earlier in my life. Unfortunately, I did not. That is, not in the same way I am learning it now. Just the words "let it go" have become the most liberating and the most important words I have learned recently. This entire experience of re-creating my life, myself, the forward thrust of who and what I'm going to be for the remainder of my days, and to do so with grace and dignity and eventually a light heart, or at least a lighter heart, is necessary to give credit to the days I've been assigned.

Each of us, obviously in the Book of Life, is scribed so many days. When the Book of Life closed on my husband it set a seal on my heart.

How to wrap my mind around the hard, unflinching reality that this year, the year 2001 of the Gregorian calendar and the year 5761 of the Hebrew calendar, this book of memory brings. For those who have gone before us are the names of my husband's grandparents, his parents and now himself. Listen to the words of the traditional prayer that one would say at the cemetery of a loved one. This is a prayer that would be said by a widow:

"Peace be upon you my man and my husband. You were the foundation of my house and the joy of my dwelling. You illuminated my darkness, but now the sun has set and I am left alone and destitute. How real are the words, how deep is the feeling, how empty, how empty."

Today, gale force winds lash the sea into a silvery foamy froth. The trees are groaning and swaying under the power. The mountain herself is huddled in a shawl of gray cloud. It is so strong, it is so powerful, it is only air, it is nature's breath, it's excessive this breath of nature. Where, oh God, was the breath I prayed for, the small frail breath of life that I so prayed for? It, too, is only air, and it was so wanting.

Approaching the observance of the anniversary of the seventh month of my husband's death, I am in the southwest part of Ireland, and we had the lowest tide in 20 years. I am taking this as an omen, and I'm hoping this is a consolation.

How do I adequately explain and do justice to all of our wonderful children? We are a blended family that has truly become an amazing amalgam of people who care for one another and fight with one another and look out for one another as is by definition, a family, a very large family.

When my husband died, the last words he said to me before going into his surgery were, "I love you." The last words he said to his son before going into surgery were, "If anything happens to me be sure you take care of Suzanne." That was a pretty heavy burden because the worst, of course, happened. I have been so blessed by the fact that my stepson Lanny, who is a highly successful financial manger, and my eldest son Jay, an entrepreneur with his own business, were willing and able to step up to the plate and say, "This is what you need to do, and this is how it needs to happen."

Lanny, following the admonition of his father, put my interest and concerns and my security and my well being as a top priority of his. There is just no way to acknowledge appropriately or thank him for all he did. He is such a mensch, he has so honored the memory of his father. My other sons, and when I use the terms sons and daughters, I am certainly including my sons-in-law and daughters-in-law, some who live out of town, of course, don't have the opportunity to do as much hands-on, but they give me moral support.

When they come to town, they look after the things in my house that need to be taken care of, they check on me and just come spend time with me. The daughters have done a role reversal. They have become the nurturers. They are the ones who in many cases have mothered and parented me, and the ability of them to do that and the willingness of them to do that has been really a remarkable, life-saving miracle for me.

I would not truly have made it without this family. Sure, there are enough people in my life so that there is always somebody available, accessible to check on me, to call, to come by, to ask me to come by, whatever. But the greatest testimonial to our marriage is this family and the continuity of this family and the incredible men and women who constitute what I lovingly refer to as "my kids". Nothing that I could say or do or write would even come close to being authentic or appropriate without acknowledging them and what they have done and their love and how much they mean to me.

Heartbeats:

• As long as you live and keep alive the memory of your loved one, they will live on in you.

• Create your own rituals and symbols as well as rely on those of your traditions, it will give transcendence to your experience.

• Give up your grudges, they imprison you.

• Recognize that guilt, shame and anger go everywhere with us and stifle our healing, let them go.

• Instead create a value for the pain in your life.

• "Nothing that is vast enters into the life of mortals without curse," said Sophocles. Would you have wanted to miss the joy to avoid this pain?

• Tell the people you love what they mean to you while they are living.

Linens and Lace

CHAPTER 11

*M*y Grandmother kept a tea-cozy, an anachronism even then. Nearly 40 years later, I happened upon such a thing in a craft shop and was flooded with memories of what it meant to be reared "lace curtain Irish" in a spick-n-span world.

The dreamer of dreams and the seer of visions are woven as woof and warp with the intensely pragmatic, in a fabric that is as crisp as Irish linen, soft and expressive as Irish lace. How enigmatic the almost preoccupation with death, coupled with the spirit to laugh life in the face. There were many virtues to which such a child ought to aspire but most especially gentility.

Somehow she knew, my unlettered grandmother, that to be bright was laudable, expected actually. To be pious without question, but to be what all of her kin yearned for and found beyond their grasp, one needed to be genteel. Grandmother had finely honed instincts for what was quality, and as far back as memory serves I can recall her pointing out to me the difference in everything from tableware to underwear. To own or possess these items was not nearly as essential as knowing the difference. As a college student majoring in sociology, I was fascinated by how true her instincts were in terms of lifestyle items that denote class, both personal and social.

Echoing in my mind is the familiar, "Suzanne," always the formal name, "when you grow up you will be a woman in possession of herself." I did not know what that meant, but it sounded grand. Women such as my grandmother were special breeds, hard as flint, for tragedy had formed them thus, yet unquestionably the heart of their families. My sainted mother was a dogma of faith, Rose Kennedy comes to mind as such a women.

At a fairly tender age, I was placed in the hands of nuns much like clay to a potter. Some were a delight, some a dread, most themselves Irish and determined to turn out the best their pedagogical and frustrated maternal instincts could produce. Never known for economy of verbiage, it seemed to take forever for these ancestors of Erin to get to the point of anything, thus allowing one the luxury of daydreaming at length before being called on to respond.

How musical and delicious was that language, it played on my soul like a harp, and I will always be grateful for my ability to take pure pleasure in the infinite arrangement of words to express both inner and outer reality. When I read something by somebody extraordinarily gifted, I will often reread over and over a certain passage or exquisite use of an adverb, much as a gourmet would desire one more taste of a perfect sauce.

Nuns always smelled wonderful, a combination of chalk and some cleaned scrubbed aroma of soap I was convinced had been milled for them alone. They glided from place to place with their beads chattering like magpies on a wire, unless, of course, they wish to surprise, in which case they held on to their beads and just appeared like some vision from another world. As the nursery rhyme goes,

"When they were good, they were very, very good, but when they were bad they were horrid."

Those of mean spirit should be left to their own anonymity but those of a genre unlike anything else deserve to be remembered. I think of my Latin teacher, who was so old and gnarled she looked like a gnome, not even five-feet tall and doing perpetual battle with her wimple, which was always askew. Still, she had the most mischievous eyes and delighted in telling jokes or puns in Latin, and always she was her own best audience. The blarney in her was as easily tapped as sugar maple trees in the spring time. Short of memory as well as stature, she routinely failed to connect names with faces so she seated us alphabetically.

For three long years I sat behind a less-than-gifted Latin scholar. Sister Aidan, growing impatient with her, would always call, "next girl, next girl." I was that next girl and have greetings in my high school annual that read, "Dear next girl." As a schoolgirl, I realized I received a hefty dose of Irish chauvinism along with the three R's.

In preparation for St. Pats', we would learn a little Irish step dancing in gym class where other students might have learned square dancing.

This protective provincialism served me well for most of my early life. I certainly grew up hearing, but was too young to have any personal recollection, of the stories I would hear from my ancestors, my family, about being in America in the early part of the 20th century, seeing signs on factories, "Help Wanted NINA" (No Irish Need Apply). It is the reason the Irish, who were a very large minority in America, developed parallel institutions with the major institutions, for instance, their own educational system, their own hospital system, charities of all kinds, youth organizations, care for the elderly, etc.

I really didn't realize that because of this protective background, that being an Irish Catholic, and female yet, was to place me in a position of being intellectually inferior in the midst of the upper class Protestant elite of American society. I was made aware of this when, as a freshman in college, I was the guest of a young man who was a student at a major Ivy League university. Now, the Ivy League universities were founded originally as religious seminaries for Protestant ministries. Most of them have little or nothing to do with their origins currently, however, that is the origin of major American educational institutions, Yale, Harvard, etc.

I was the date of someone who was very bright, very gifted and had a promising future. The mother of his roommate took him aside, and yet within ear shot of me, informed him how disappointed she was to see that he would appear at this event with someone who was such a social liability. I started looking all around and thinking, "Who could this social liability possibly be?" Then I realized I was the social liability because I was Irish and Catholic.

That was my very first experience of living what most minority people experience in a majority culture. It wasn't until a few years later, when John F. Kennedy was running for president of the United States, that it was thought he could not become President because of his being a Catholic. And had he not come to Houston and made a very convincing case to the Baptist ministers that the pope would not be running America, we probably still would have never had a Catholic president, and to date we have had only one.

There has yet to be a Jewish president, although certainly in the last presidential election with Joseph Lieberman running as a vice presidential candidate we certainly have come infinitely closer than we had when I was a child and as a young woman.

It's a circuitous route for me to be in Ireland, reflecting on much of what my early life was like, how I got from where I was to where I am, and in a sense the returning back. I feel a kinship here because I know the culture as one who experiences it through an immigrant experience. It is presumptuous to say I understand Irish culture from being in Ireland two, three, four or six months a year because I do not. I don't live here all the time. I have second- and third-hand information and experience, but it certainly serves me well in the circumstances. Being a person of faith and religion was always very important to me even though I have struggled with my relationship with God for long as I can remember. It matters to me. So the experience of coming from what I was, this very devout Irish Catholic girl, to becoming in my mid-30's a traditional practicing Jew is quite a journey indeed.

In my normal course of life, I don't talk about it a whole lot because it was something that happened so far back now, nearly half my life ago, that I don't think about it. However, it certainly has a bearing and a relevance on who I am, how my life turned out to be the kind of life that it did, how my marriage with Larry occurred.

Had I not, in my early and mid-30s, undergone a real crises of faith and a real search for an adult religious experience, things would have been much different. What's important is that it worked for me, and I stress for me, because often times people who have converted from something to something else approach it with a kind of missionary zeal that says, "You are wrong, I am right, I have seen the light and all must do likewise."

I find that so arrogant and so inappropriate that I want to be sure and go on public record as saying the decisions I made for myself were personal and for me alone. I don't think everyone should do what I did, I don't think that it's for everyone, and, of course, I don't think there is anything wrong with being what you were raised, etc., etc. It simply didn't work for me. As a young woman, and by young I am thinking late 20's, early 30's, which seemed very grown up at the time but so young to me now, I was very much an activist in social causes. What I found was that, overwhelmingly, the number of folks involved in these causes, be they civil rights, anti-war, were Jewish people, and that was of great interest to me because I have always felt that what you do is infinitely more important than what you say.

So in the course of my social activism and concomitant with that was my own search for and understanding of religion as an adult. You learn things as a kid that can serve you very well but comes a point at which, if you wish to take ownership of anything, you need to examine it and find out what it means for you. What I found by studying the gospels was that I was drawn back into the historical understanding of what it would have meant to be alive at the time of Jesus. What was the climate, what was the Jewish environment, what was the early Christian environment? After all, people weren't really even considered Christians for perhaps a hundred years until after Jesus had lived and died. It was one of many sects or ways of being Jewish.

As I began to explore that, I began to become far more knowledgeable with what is referred to as the Old Testament or Hebrew Scriptures. As I personally became more aware of that and more knowledgeable about that, I felt the value system was a very sound and a very good one, and the original arrangement that God had made with Moses, the original covenant, this was okay. The Abraham relationship, the Moses relationship, those were very sound relationships. I could deal with those and, because all of the Christian later experiences and traditions were based on that, there was a vague familiarity but not great. What I discovered for myself was that, if one can no longer accept the Christian interpretation of the story of The Garden, if one no longer accepts, in other words, the concept of original sin, then you have a problem with the need for a personal Redeemer.

If one does not have original sin, one doesn't have the need to be redeemed from original sin. So the whole domino theory of the need for the Jesus person as part of the God experience was no longer relevant for me. This is a very short and simplified way of explaining what took many, many years and lots of study and lots of discussion and lots of research and lots of anguish to come up with. I do remember a couple of events that significantly impacted my decision, and one was being in church at Mass for the baptism of a child for whom I was the godmother.

It was at Easter time, and the sermon spoke about the apostles being in hiding from "the Jews." Now, they were Jews, too, so that just struck me as being so peculiar. That would be like saying I was a person who had been a political activist as an American anti-war demonstrator, for instance, and I was in hiding from "the Americans." It made no sense. I might have been hiding from the FBI, I might have been hiding from the CIA, but Americans was a generic term that included everybody, especially me. I would have also been an American.

Jesus and the apostles would have been Jews and have known themselves as nothing other than Jews. My immediate impression was to sit up rather directly and take notice of the fact that this was a means of separating out what became the Christian experience from the early Jewish experience. It just made it very clear to me that I simply could no longer accept this particular religious belief system.

Someone asked me many, many years later in my life, "What do you tell people when they look at you and say, you're Jewish?" I say, "Well, I was raised an Irish Catholic, and I am still Irish." He laughed, but it is the reality of my life. I will always be this blend of two cultures.

In many ways I probably have the advantage of getting the best of both worlds. Finally I reached the time when I needed to see a rabbi because I had been weighing and weighing this for many, many years and finally thought, I really need to get on with it; either I need to do something about it or I need to forget it. I asked my closest friend at the time if she would introduce me to a rabbi since I really didn't know one and certainly couldn't just pick up the phone book and pick out one and go and see him. She said, yes, she would introduce me to her rabbi, but he was a little skeptical, and I certainly understand why he was, about what I wanted and who I was and so on. He told her he would see me and would give me 15 minutes.

At the time she was a very heavy smoker, and he kept me for an hour, and I have visions of her pacing in the parking lot smoking one cigarette after another thinking, surely something dreadful must have happened to me in this meeting with this rabbi. It was a wonderful meeting, and I will forever be grateful to him because he set me on a path that was not only a very well-rounded piece of advice for what I was undergoing but great life advice, and one doesn't often get great life advice. He asked me, among other things, if I realized what I would be giving up. I knew this conversation was about Christmas and Easter, etc.

I said, yes, I certainly did and had thought a great deal about that. But since I view these not as cultural secular expressions as much of society does but really as religious expressions, then I wasn't really giving them up because they no longer held the meaning and the significance for me they once had. He was okay with that but I must have begun to smile or smirk because he said to me, "nu?"

I said, "Well, rabbi, as you know I come from an Irish background so giving up St. Pat's, that party, would really be tough." He was wonderful, he didn't miss a lick, he didn't bat an eye and he said, "I don't know why you should, I didn't."

Now, of course, I was the one taken back. It seems this man had been a professor at Loyola University, which is in St. Louis and is staffed by Jesuits. I knew we were having good communication when he kept referring to the Jesuits as "the Jesi's this and the Jesi's that." He told me that his relatives had come from Dublin and that he was related to the Briscoe family, who had had two lord mayors of Dublin amongst their families. He said they came to visit him when he was in St. Louis, and that you have heard nothing until you have heard the Torah chanted with a brogue. He said, "I would not ask you to give up the green beer but I might ask you to give up Mass in the morning."

I thought this was a very fair and equitable exchange. He also gave me a very large and comprehensible reading list, which I dutifully attacked because that was an easy thing to do. Then he said a couple of things to me that were very significant; he said, "Look, I am not the person to start with you." This by the way was an orthodox rabbi. "I am not the place for you to start. I am going to send you to a colleague of mine who will provide you with a good Jewish background and an entry that will be much more appropriate for you."

He said to me, "You need to call this rabbi and tell him I gave you his name and that I said he should take you on as a private student because you already know too much to be put in the class." Now this is what in Yiddish is called Chutzpah. I went ahead and called the rabbi and said, "Rabbi Y. said that you should see me and this is why." I think out of sheer curiosity the man must have wanted to see me and thought, "Who could this woman possibly be that would have the nerve to do such a thing?" where, of course, I thought I was just following directions.

The other thing that the rabbi said to me was not to try to do everything all at once because I would fail and be overwhelmed. He said to try to do things little by little and grow incrementally. For instance, at some point I may wish to keep a kosher home. At that time I had no intention of keeping a kosher home, however, he was right, the time did come.

He said, "Don't try to do it all at once. Think of it, the whole of the Jewish experience, as an overcoat. You will try it on and if it fits, you will wear it. If it doesn't fit, you wait. You'll try it on another time, you'll try another coat."

I thought this was also very good advice. He also said not to go discussing what you're going to be doing with everyone you know. Everyone will have an opinion and may place you in a position where you will feel obligated to go through with a conversion that you may ultimately decide, after you undergo the courses and the classes, that you don't wish to do. Don't paint yourself in that kind of a box.

I thought those were very, very good life lessons, to try to grow, to do things gradually so as not to paint myself into a box, not to blow my horn and let everybody know what I'm doing. He said, "You don't want to feel as if you're stuck with it in case you change your mind."

I did all of the things he suggested, went to see his colleague who did take me on as a private student, who did prepare me for an adult bat mitzvah. I did learn to read Hebrew and chant the Torah, and I was the first adult female in that congregation to do so, a factor of which I take a certain amount of pride. I joked about the fact that, when I was this adult bat mitzvah, not only did I have to prepare the cookies, I had to chant the Torah at the same time. I was the bat mitzvah kid and the mother of such, at the very same event.

My friends were terrific, they prepared me, they coached me, they cheered me on, and my family was there. They were supportive, I am sure wondering in many cases, "What is she doing?" Nonetheless, they were there, and they were supportive, and they were encouraging. So I was thusly launched into the world of a Jewish experience. Like anything else, when you want to do something, of course, you work at it a whole lot harder, so the learning of the tradition and the learning of the observance and the history, that was not so hard, frankly.

What becomes very, very difficult is the acculturation. This is not just simply going from being a Methodist to becoming a Presbyterian, this is moving into a whole new culture, and that is what took years and years and years to be able to be at home in and to feel a part of. The fact that I was made aware of that, and knew it was going to be a process, and it wouldn't happen automatically was helpful. When I could make a joke in Yiddish, when I could make a pun in Yiddish, I realized, uh huh, I have arrived. I can say and do things culturally that I would never have thought possible.

That had a great deal to do with my eventual and very gradual acculturation into being Jewish. Now I have this Irish Catholic background co-mingling with this American Jewish cultural experience, which makes for one, I would say, very unique and certainly a life-enriching total experience and total package.

When I was a child and through most of my early adult life, I lived in the northeast of America. That is a place where you experience seasons. Having lived as long as I have in the south, I miss seasons, I miss the change of season, I miss seeing the first flowers of spring and the first scarlet leaves of the autumn and the first snowflakes. Periodically, my mission would be to make a pilgrimage up north so that I could see winter or see a little autumn color. Of all of the seasons, however, autumn would be described for me as the favorite season of the year.

I think about that now because it is the autumn of my life. Autumn is the time of the year when things begin to go into their deep winter sleep, the preparation for the winter sleep where things germinate and prepare to come back in the spring. Now I find that I have to think about that and think about going into the winter of my soul and what that will mean for me. It is an interesting exercise; after all, I had never expected to be alone at this stage of my life. The odds were I would be alone at some time in my life but I had visualized that perhaps as being another 20 years down the road.

It didn't happen for me that way, so now I am in the process of creating or recreating the who of me, the what of me. No longer important is the what-will-you-do-when-you-grow-up question, but what will you do with the remainder of your life that is meaningful to you and contributory to not just one's immediate family but to society as a whole.

Certainly 10 months ago, when I was in such shock, it would never have even occurred to me that there was the possibility I could be making a contribution to anything. My big concern was simply to get up in the morning and put one foot in front of the other. The thought and realization now that I can teach an occasional class, I can do an occasional workshop, I can become involved in cultural events and committee work I find meaningful, is a great gift because I truly never thought I would be able to do that again. Not that I wasn't capable but I would not have the desire, the initiative, the ability to get outside of myself and get into what is important for a larger community.

The gift of being able to come to my Irish house and really sort of hole up here at the edge of the world and think about and reflect on what has happened, where I am now, where I need to go from here, has been very, very life-saving for me. Shortly after I returned to America after my last visit to Ireland, I realized how important it was for me to be at home in Houston for Halloween for the funniest of reasons actually.

Halloween was a gift that the Irish brought in large measure to America, and they got it from their Druidic ancestors. The world of the Irish is one in which mythology and reality are very, very loosely connected. The veil between the land of the living and the land of the dead is one that is very delicately woven, and souls pass between those two worlds at particular times.

The one time of the year that it was particularly celebrated was at the end of October and the first of November. Interestingly enough, when the Christians came to Ireland and really piggybacked off the local customs, which was very smart, they made the first of November All Saints Day. That was a hollowed day, a holy day, so Halloween was the Hallowed Eve before All Saints Day. Halloween was the night that people were concerned or afraid because spirits rose from their graves, traveled the world, and they looked for their lost bodies and for other people to inhabit and so on and so forth.

The Druid had a tradition of placing a little candle, a little light of some sort, inside a hollowed out turnip to scare away the goblins and whatever. Eventually, waves and waves of these people began to observe this custom in America. But since we do everything bigger and better we use pumpkins instead, which we carve out as jack-o'-lantern faces to scare away the evil spirits. The old tradition, the Druidic tradition, was to set out soul cakes so that those on their journey from one world to the next would have some provisions and hence we go door to door and now beg for Halloween treats.

We moved into our Houston house on the weekend of Halloween. Foolishly, I accepted for us an invitation for a costume party that night. I was truly not thinking clearly when I did this because we were dead tired from the move, but we had the costumes, we were dressed, and we were ready to go. We also totally forgot that kids would be coming to the door for trick-or-treat, and I had no candy, no provisions, no nothing.

This house has an intercom system so that when you push the front doorbell it rings through the telephone and you can talk to somebody through the speaker, it is very snazzy. We were dressing for this party, and the bell kept ringing and these little kids would come trick-or-treat. All we could do was explain we were so sorry but had just moved in and didn't have anything. One little kid, who sounded to be three or four, came to the door and rang the buzzer trick-or-treating. My husband, who by now felt just awful because he had nothing, explained in great length to this little kid that we had just moved in and we didn't have any candy. He told him that if he would come back tomorrow, we would go to the store and we would get him a lot of good things tomorrow.

Of course, when you are three or four, tomorrow doesn't cut it, the day of Halloween was the day of Halloween. The little kid said, okay and went off about his business. When we came home from this party, we walked past the front door and noticed that inside the mail slot this little kid had left a Milky Way and a dime. He had felt so sorry for my husband because he had felt so bad about not having any goodies for Halloween that he actually gave some goodies to him. I think about that every single Halloween, what a darling, darling thing that was, and that this kid has grown up now.

I think also about how easy it was for Larry to trigger that sort of response in almost anybody. He could make people want to help him, and want to do things for him, and want to cooperate with him. That is a real talent. He didn't have to coerce people into getting them to do what he wanted them to do, he could by sheer force of his own personality and in this case, a genuine concern for somebody else. He could have people do for him things that in many cases they would do for probably few if any other people.

So on Halloween, I wanted to be in that house. I wanted to be there having that memory of what it was like the day we came back from that Halloween party and there was the candy and the dime that little boy had left because he felt so badly about Larry not having any Halloween trick-or-treat candy. It always makes me chuckle.

After Halloween, we begin to gear up for Thanksgiving, and, of course, in America people start gearing up for Christmas, we start doing that shortly after the Forth of July. It seems every year it gets earlier and earlier. Thanksgiving in our family this year was a mixed blessing. We were all there, and that was wonderful because I felt the need of family. I was finally able to cook a big enough meal for everybody and not feel overwhelmed or burdened by that. I wanted so much for the grandchildren to have that kind of continuity of experience. If everything in their life changes in relation to their grandparents, that is a terrible, terrible loss, and I think the ability for them to see the continuity of events such as having a Thanksgiving family gathering was very important for them and for us.

It's important to note here that the grandchildren are all little kids. They are wired, they've been together all day, they've been running around, they haven't napped, they're up the stairs they're down the stairs, etc., and they're yelling and so on. Around eight o'clock, my youngest stepdaughter Sheila, looked at me and said, "If dad were here, he'd have a heart attack." Then we started to laugh and we both said, "Well, been there done that." Now, macabre as that sounds that sort of thing allowed us to have a really good laugh, and that is a very, very important thing to be able to do.

One of the funny things Leslie said about Larry was that he had a shelf life of about 12 minutes when it came to being with all these little kids because it overwhelmed him so. They were everywhere. He loved them, he really adored them, but he had to take them in small doses. When there was everybody all over the place and all over him, sometimes it was more than he could take. We laughed about that because he probably would laugh about it, too.

I remember that the previous year, which turned out to be his last Thanksgiving, we had the five oldest grandchildren spend the night. When I say the five oldest grandchildren, I'm talking about three seven-year-olds, a four-year-old and an eight-year-old. We are not talking about grown up people. They slept on the third floor, and we slept on the second floor and, of course, all we could here was this pitter patter of little feet running back and forth and back and forth and lots of giggling and lots of silliness. Larry kept saying, "When are those kids going to go to sleep?" I said, "Eventually, trust me they will get tired, they will go to sleep."

Well, finally, he'd had it with them so he went to the foot of the stairs and said, "If I have to come up there, I am going to put you all in the car and take you home." Fortunately, that did it, nobody called his bluff. As he was just sort of easing himself back into bed, I said to him, "I'm so glad you said *you* are going to take them in the car and *you* are going to take them home because I have to promise you, after cooking for all these folks, I am not getting out of my jammys, putting these kids in the car and taking them home."

As luck would have it, they went to sleep. The next morning, at the request of the children, we went to I HOP for breakfast. That was easy because those who wanted pancakes could have pancakes, those who wanted eggs could have eggs. About 9:30, my husband looked at his watch and said to me, "Can I take them home now?" I said, "Yes, you may take them home now." So he'd been a wonderful grandfather, he had a lot of fun with them, he had taken them out for breakfast. But he'd had it with the grandparenting for a while, and now it was time to take them home.

I was so happy we were able to do that because that is the one and only time that they will all get to do that with him, so it is a perfect example of the seize-the-moment kind of idea. Don't let the opportunity to do something fun or spontaneous or impromptu with your family come and go because you really never know how many opportunities you will have to do that. I think about that, of course, every waking day and in most of my sleep. I think about my husband but much of it is remembering or recalling. However, there are moments, and they're not even moments, they're nano-seconds, when I am not remembering something I'm truly experiencing him, I am hearing him.

We have a musician friend who cut a CD that included a piece written for another mutual musician friend of Larry's who had died. When I listen to that, it just brings tears to my eyes because the cycle or circle of loss and death is just so great. When Larry first heard that piece, I could hear him keeping kind of a rhythm like he was the drummer to that. I could hear it, and all of a sudden I looked up fully expecting to see him doing that because I could truly hear him do that.

There are moments when it isn't a remembering, it's a tangible palpable presence, and those are wonderful moments. They almost take your breath away, you take a deep gasp because he's really, really there. It is just a fleeting tiny, tiny fragment of a second but, nonetheless, there is that second of when he is there.

I was preparing things for Hannuka when I was remembering, and suddenly he was there, he was just there. It's an odd sort of a feeling, but it is a wonderfully reassuring feeling that someone you have loved is never really, really gone in the sense that they're a part of you. It isn't just the good stuff that is a part of you, everything that was about them is a part of you, and the ability to identify that totality does not die because they don't automatically become a saint. The things that were frustrating about them when they were alive are the very same things that they took with them to the grave. That didn't change. But, to deny those is to deny in a very real way, the human.

We have had several grandchildren born to our family since my husband died, and the pathos of that realization that these are children he will never know and will never know him is real. It's a lot of joy because these are beautiful, healthy children for whom we can all say grace and be so thankful. It is also a lot of sadness because we know they won't know Pepa, and Pepa will never know them. These children are named for him in one capacity or another so that they will have as part of their personal personality genetic code the imprint of their grandfather, not only in their genes but also in their name and in their memories of him, and this will be impressed upon them as they grow. They're beautiful children, and he would be so proud of them. In some way I feel he is proud of the children, the grandchildren, of all of us for doing what it is we're doing to get on with our lives under a lot of stress and a lot of loss.

The founding of this new life, this new way to be alive, I guess, would be acceptable because people do it to just kind of go on with what you had done only doing it as a single person. I find that that is inadequate to the task. I have to find a new path and a new way to be who I'm going to be for the rest of my remaining years.

On the day of the anniversary of my husband and I being introduced, of our meeting, that was the day I knew he was going to die. I was informed that the damage was irreparable, and on that day I put his wedding ring on a chain around my neck. I wore it everyday for that year. At the end of that year, it was okay for me to remove the ring, not because I wanted to be free of it, but because it was important for me to create rituals and events that would allow me to move from one stage to the next. It was important for me to be able to say that, from the day I knew of his dying for sure, for one year, I would wear his wedding ring, as well as my own, but I would wear his ring around my neck.

Heartbeats:

• Do some inner space exploration of yourself, your past and your memories, you may get to know you better.

• Don't try to do it all at once, you'll get there eventually.

• Never miss a chance to make a memory, it may never come again.

• Tell your story to your kids and grandkids. Don't be afraid to laugh.

• Smile because it happened rather than cry because it's over.

The Call of Ireland

CHAPTER 12

*H*ow ever did we end up with a home in Ireland? It seems a most unique place for people, one of whom is not Irish, neither of whom are Catholic, in a country that is 99 percent plus, I believe, Catholic. How ever did we end up in Ireland with this fabulous home and this dream of retirement in this beautiful spot? It is a wonderful saga, actually, of how life can be so serendipitous, how if we're open to possibilities, life can give us wonderful surprises. In the early '90's, probably 1990, maybe 1991 at the latest, I was in the process of completing my doctoral program. I was in a program that permitted study at various universities all over the world that was part of this collegial program they offered.

One of the opportunities was to study in Ireland with a woman who was going to be the visiting professor, a woman from Georgetown University, who I knew to be very good at what she did. She was teaching a course on the scriptural images of woman in art. I thought this would be a fascinating topic, and since I was doing this degree in religious studies, I thought this would be a unique opportunity, both to study with her and to have a whole additional insight into the subject. So I filled out the application and was accepted and was off to Ireland.

It was going to be my opportunity to go to the place of my forbearers. In my naïveté I thought, surely I would have all kinds of opportunity to look up my relatives, travel the country, etc. When one is part of a program like this, where you have to condense so much information and so much work in a fairly short period of time, you don't go any place. You get up at 7:30 in the morning, you work until 11 o'clock at night, you stay onsite, and you do what you are there to do. I loved it, and it was a wonderful experience. The information I have learned has certainly served me well.

But, I wasn't exactly tootling around, viewing the country and tracking down lost relatives. So I suggested to Larry that he might like to come over for a week and we'd rent a car and drive around Ireland. He thought that would be great, it would be a little vacation for the two of us, so he did that. Now this is a person of Russian-German ancestry without, as far as we know, a drop of Irish blood flowing through his veins. Blarney, yes! Blood, no! He got to Ireland and got about as far as the outskirts of Shannon Airport, which is not the garden spot of Ireland, I must tell you, and he fell in love with the place. If ever there was a love at first sight, it was Larry and Ireland. Every place we went in the country he loved it, it was beautiful, it was fabulous, I must have a place here, etc.

We made the trip to Ireland every year for the next several years and really visited and drove most of the country. The interesting thing is that it's a very little country, and the people who live here, by and large, don't travel much. They travel to Spain, but they don't travel much in Ireland. So you would ask somebody in Galway where is someplace that is maximum 20 miles away, and they would look at you blank, they'd never heard of it, they didn't know where it was, etc. I often wonder where my father's resistance to moving or traveling more than five miles within his place of origin comes from, now I know.

We had the wonderful experience of traveling down the east coast, down the peninsulas, up the west coast. We stayed in Connemara, in the Midlands, in Waterford, and certainly always a trip to Dublin for shopping and theater and just the buzz that comes with being in such a currently hot spot as Dublin.

We always had a fondness for the southwest part of the country, for the southwest part of Cork, actually. It's rugged, unspoiled, mountainous, it's craggy, it's primitive, it's isolated, it's drop-dead gorgeous, and it is not touristy. That was a big plus because having to negotiate around all those tourists in those goofy little T-shirts that have somebody's name on them so they don't lose each other en route is not the sort of thing one has any desire to do. Worse than that is negotiating the huge buses on these very tiny roads or going into a restaurant or a local pub only to be overwhelmed by tourists.

This is coming from a person who is herself not native and sounding very chauvinistic. However, I have put my money where my mouth is and feel I can make a tiny complaint with having to deal with the excessive tourism. We had American friends who had an ancestral home on the Beara Peninsula. We visited them because we liked them and want to see them and because Pat had always said, "You've really not seen Ireland until you have come to my part of Ireland."

He just happened to be right, so we would go every year to visit the O'Learys and spend time on the Beara. The more we spent time there, the more we decided that truly this would be a wonderful place to have a home. Now that's an easier-said-than-done statement. To give you a tiny bit of insight into what this part of Ireland is like, we decided for sure that we were going to look for a piece of property before we left, this particular trip. We were talking with Pat about this on a Friday.

On Saturday we were told that his cousin had some ideas. By Sunday, his cousin had found the farmer from whom we purchased the land, the site, and we had gotten these all in alignment. That wouldn't be so surprising if the cousin were a real estate agent, but he most certainly is not. Not only is he not, he doesn't have a telephone and is so shy he won't even come into his own cousin's house to talk to you.

So since there are no secrets in the country of Ireland at all, and since the idea of privacy is really a totally foreign concept, once the word was out that the Americans were looking for a place to buy property it was a done deal. All you needed to do, of course, was have the word go out at Mass, which is the local community center.

We had seen this spot at the base of Hungry Hill. Hungry Hill is a very large mountain, the scene actually of Daphne du Maurier's novel of the same name, *The Hungry Hill*. Its claim to fame, aside from its beauty, I suppose, is the fact that on the other side of the mountain, in a little town called Allihies, is a famous copper mine, or it was at one time in the last century before it was destroyed. Also, there is a magnificent beach that is purely the result of the extraction from this copper mine.

Our particular spot is on a ledge at the base of this mountain overlooking the Atlantic. It is an incredible view. There isn't a place in the whole house that you don't look at mountains or meadow or sheep or the Atlantic. It is a slow day when you can't sit in your living room and look out at the water and see trawlers from all over the world trawling literally up and down just out your front door. It's an amazing spot.

The house happened to be built on a rock foundation because it truly is at the base of this mountain. That was okay, it looked like a good solid place, and it's going no place. But, what happens is, in Ireland, when you decide to build in what is known as the Green Belt, that is the place between the sea and the road, you need to have planning permission, very carefully considered by the County council. That makes sense to me because I live in a city that has no zoning, and I can see the infinite wisdom of being a lot more cautious about your resources, and truly the topography, the scenery is what is gorgeous about this place. It is a fishing community, a small farming community, lots of sheep, but that's it. So if the natural beauty were to be spoiled, it would be a great (loss), not only to the loveliness of the place but to the economic survival.

We submitted our plans and arranged to deal with the architect who had been the architect for our friend's home and who did lovely work that was in keeping with the genre of where we would be living. He also had the advantage of being the outgoing president of the county's environmental association so he knew the drill and he knew the rules, which proved to be really, really valuable.

Anyway, we submitted our plan and we waited and we waited and we waited some more. There was always a little glitch, a little complication, a little whatever. One of the little complications was that the house would be situated in such a way that the elevation would be too high for the environmental association. In other words, you could see the house from either the sea or, obviously more important, from the road behind. You are unaware of how many people would live in an area because everybody is kind of nestled down behind a rock or in a little hole or valley.

This is done for a number of reasons: to protect the home from the severe winds and weather, to protect the view and to protect the landscape. Okay, that was a doable. However, in order to achieve what the council said we needed to do, we had to have four-and-a-half million pounds of stone removed to lower this place something like five feet from its original site. That's a lot of stone to be moved. But saying that this could be done and then the actual doing is another thing all together. The plans for the house, the actual physical plans for the house were acceptable, and that was a good thing.

The percolation, which means you have to check the ground for where you're going to put your well and where you are going to put your bio-cycle system, etc., was another issue. It took quite a long time to negotiate how all of that was going to work. All of this, of course, while we were in one country and the house under discussion was in another country. The long and the short of it is that after about a year, and this was a rush job, we got permission to build this house.

In the ensuing summer, however, we decided that perhaps we ought to look at some other possibilities. If permission were denied, we would have wasted a whole year and we would be starting this drill all over again. So the thought was to look at homes that were already in existence, homes that were for sale, that may have needed to be gutted and rehabbed or whatever. Or we might look for a piece of property that already had building permission on it because there are sites that already come with building approval on them. This particular site on which we built did not because it had been zoned for farming only.

To make that change required nothing short of an act of God. So we decided to go with a local realtor and look at places that were on the market or places that had the potential for being built upon. None was as beautiful as the place we already had our eye on, but we were doing some reality testing here. In wonderful, wonderful Irish fashion, Pat O'Leary's mother, who was then around 90 and who had grown up in this neighborhood – their home had been her home – suggested that we look at a certain place on Hungry Hill.

The realtor said, "Well, Mrs. O'Leary, it is a very nice place but it isn't for sale."

She said, "It will be because the man has died, and his widow is from England and is not happy here and she is going." Then she suggested another house. "Now, did you look at the pink house?"

"Well, that is a very nice house also Mrs. O'Leary, but it's not for sale."

"Well, it will be because they're not going to be staying here, they are going to be moving someplace else."

This was information to which the realtor was not privy. When we were in the car Larry said, "How does she know all this stuff?"

I said, "Well, she grew up here, everyone in this village is related to everyone else, but most importantly she goes to Mass on Sunday, and that's where she gets all of her news. She doesn't have to go anyplace else but to the Sunday Mass and she gets all of her news."

Sunday Mass in this little village is something out of a movie. You see old men standing outside at the very edge of the road and just outside of the church, having their last cigarette of the morning, the very, very senior citizens, by which I mean people in their 80's and 90's.

The lifestyle here must lead people to live forever. When you see people who looked to be well in to their 80's bicycling up these hills on a plain old bicycle with no gears, you can understand why they might live forever, despite the smoking and the high consumption of dairy products and cholesterol, etc. Whatever it is they take in, certainly they work off. These are the fellows who hang around until the very last moment so they are the last people in to church and the first people out of church.

One of them, who was Mrs. O'Leary's contemporary, asked her when she was going to be leaving. She said, "I'm sorry to say I'll be leaving tomorrow."

He said, "Well, you can't come back until you leave."

Isn't that a wonderful, wonderful perspective on life? When we talk about something moving at a fairly slow pace in Texas where we're from, we talk about the mañana mentality because we live close to Mexico and we have a lot of opportunities to interface with Mexican culture. In Ireland mañana would be aggressive.

I cannot explain how the concept of time is so entirely different and unique. It is really wonderful once you get with it, but it always takes me at least a week of being here to de-program myself from being on American time and an American schedule and getting onto an Irish time and Irish schedule, which is essentially no schedule at all.

In the winter, people don't get up particularly early, I'm not sure they do in the summer either, but they certainly don't in the winter because it is dark until 8 or 8:30 in the morning, then it is dark again at 5 o'clock in the afternoon. So the days are very short, the nights are very long, and it gives one much, much opportunity to spend time in pubs and visiting with folks.

In the summer, the days are very long, beginning about 4:30 in the morning, and it doesn't really get dark until 10:30 or 11 at night. In fact, there are times when it really never gets pitch dark, there's always a kind of glow in the sky in the summer time. On a summer day in Ireland, one would expect to spend a certain amount of time moseying around the countryside, but also you would anticipate that you would either be called upon by friends and neighbors or you would call upon friends and neighbors. Therefore, I always feel it incumbent upon myself to have something freshly baked available because people will show up.

I am, truthfully, in a house at the edge of the world, and that is not an exaggeration. I could be in Houston, Texas, for days and weeks on end and never have as many people just appear for one thing or another as I have here. This is not an easy place to even locate, but everyone who lives here knows everyone who is here or lives here. The opportunity to visit with someone or to have someone who has done some work on your house to drop by to check on something, etc., is truly a wonderful way to exist, to spend your time.

As we were now contemplating that we were going to have approval, we finally did after almost a year, we did get planning permission to build the house, which was a very big thing because I am told there are people who have waited years, literally. I don't think I have years at this stage of my life to wait. Planning permission was granted, and now we were about to begin. The coordination of all of this was an incredible undertaking.

The architect and the general contractor and the land contractor and Larry were all having perpetual powwows as to what has to happen first and when does this occur and so on and so forth. It gets even dicier because if you're going to talk to somebody in Ireland at 9 o'clock in the morning, you have to be talking in Houston at 3 o'clock in the morning. So my husband would be up many a night, in the middle of the night, having conferences, sometimes from the site because something would come up, and they would need to know what do we do?

It is an amazing experience, certainly it is novel, to decide that the time has come when you need to pick out the fixtures for your house, by which I mean your sink and your refrigerator and your stove and your plumbing. I knew what I wanted this house to look like, I knew what I wanted the kitchen, particularly, to look like, therefore, I was very particular about what was going to happen in this house and in that kitchen.

The person who did the cabinetwork is by profession a furniture maker, so the cabinets are amazing. They are so finely crafted that there are no nails in the drawers, they are all beachwood dove tailed and lined in maple. They're just beautiful; you almost don't want to put something in them because they are so lovely. This, however, was a very long procedure. It seemed one could have constructed something on the order of the Empire State Building in less time than it was taking to put together that kitchen.

Even more complicated was the stairway. We had designed a stair that is an open stair in the sense that, where other stairways have those little spindles between the banister and the base of the stairs, this was going to be with heavy, heavy glass. It turned out to be a beautiful idea because there is a skylight above it, and it shines through, and it's lovely. The person doing this had never done a stairway before. He felt with great confidence he could, and he did, but this in itself was a true hair-tearing experience.

When we decided it was time to pick the appliances, I did so in Dublin because I knew the greatest selection for everything was going to be in Dublin. It is nothing short of strange to go into a series of showrooms and to decide what it is you're going to ultimately be able to do and to pick out every sink, every faucet, every toilet, every everything you're going to need in this house in one day. That's the way it was because that's when I was there and that's when it had to happen.

I had the good sense to hire a driver, through the hotel where we were staying, who knew the city because Dublin is a very difficult city to get around. There is no place to park, and the traffic is awful. If you can get a taxi, you might be able to get him to take you someplace but you'd never get him to come back and pick you up. In order for me to be able to get from one part of the city to the next, I needed to have somebody who knew the city so I wouldn't be crisscrossing, someone who could get me to where I needed to go in the most efficient way and would wait for me and take me to the next place. I found everything we needed, which is pretty remarkable, and began to place the orders.

Louise Kennedy, a woman who has become a rather renowned designer there, bought and restored this incredible Georgian on Merion Square in Dublin. I guess she'd be the Donna Karan of Ireland. I really wanted to see it, I'd seen pictures of it so I made an appointment to go there to purchase some of her clothing and, hence, I would have an opportunity to see this incredible restored Georgian. I had never met the woman and didn't know what she looked like, but I was so impressed with the person who was doing the fittings, I thought to myself, "This women really knows what she's doing."

Well, of course she did, because she was the person who designed the clothes so she certainly was capable of making the fittings. More to the point for me was that, in the course of being there,

I was able to explain to her that we were in Ireland because we were building a house here. She said she had just restored this Georgian, and she really knew the best people for supplies and, if there were any contacts she could make for me, she would be more than happy to do so, which I thought was a very lovely gesture.

She did recommend a certain tile supply place that was able to locate exactly what we wanted. We wanted very large Italian tiles, something like 18- or 19-inch square, for most of the first floor with the exception of our bedroom, which is hardwood. The whole rest of the first floor was this tile. Because it was such a very big space, we didn't want them to be small tiles and really look busy. We had been having a great deal of difficulty finding the right size and the right color tile.

I went to her suggested spot and, sure enough, there it was. One of the benefits of being in a place as small as Ireland is that everyone knows, somehow, how to be connected to everyone else and everything else, and how to enable you to get what it is you need. We had picked out the things we needed. I had the colors for the interior, working with a wonderful woman who really knew her business. She had found someone to do what in Ireland is called soft furnishings, which would be window covers and bedspreads and that sort of thing.

So we were off and running. We also had to find another person in another shop in another part of the country to supply the carpeting because that had to happen on the second floor. And it just goes on and on, all of the things you think about in building a house, which are innocents abroad. We had never built a house any place. So fools rush in because we didn't know. In this case ignorance <u>was</u> bliss. Had we known then what we know now, we probably wouldn't have had the nerve to do it but we did. We just figured, "We can do this."

Each phase of a house under construction is predicated upon the previous stage being completed or at least in such a condition that you can build upon it. One of the typical examples of what happened in this project involved the radiant heating setup under the first floor. Hot water is heated by propane gas, but the propane tank had not been delivered and installed because the area in which it was suppose to go had not been carved out of this rocky crevasse, and the cement apron had not been poured. There had been much discussion, not always amicable, and disagreement about where it was supposed to go and how it was suppose to go there. Consequently nothing was happening.

Weeks were going along and nothing was happening. Now it's sort of a thing for want of a nail, etc. Until we could get heat – and until we had a gas tank, no heat – and run the heat for at least two weeks, we couldn't finish with interior plaster, and you couldn't even consider the possibility of painting.

The walls in this house are two feet thick, and they're cinder block and stone. It takes a long time in what sometimes seems like the wettest country in the world for something to dry out sufficiently so you can plaster and paint without fear of it all crumbling or buckling. Therefore, the heat, the installation of and the operation of the heat, was a big, important issue. Finally, after untold discussions, and because at this point Larry had said, "You've got to go, Suzanne, and just be there to deal with it," we were able to get it done.

The gas company brought the gas tank and left it at the top of the road, just deposited it there, just left it. Now we had to get someone to come bring the gas tank from the road to the spot, have it connected, get the water going, get the gas going and get the place heated before we could do anything else.

This is one tiny little glitch, one example of what it's like to be building a house here. This is an Irish equivalent of a year in Provence, writ large because we are a very long way from anything. That's the good part, the beautiful part, that you are a good long way from anything.

That's also the not-so-good-part because, after all, everything has to be brought in. Electricity had to be brought in, and when I say brought in I mean the poles and the wires, and then we had to have the holes dug, and we are talking solid rock. The water well went nearly 400 hundred feet deep before we got to sufficient good water.

The television was something Larry wanted very much to have, but I did not. He was right, most especially since I am here by myself much of the time now, and to be without the television would be truly dreary. Since world events are such that you really can't be away for any length of time and not know what's going on in the world, the television is wonderful.

The television dish is someplace up in the gorse, which is this very deceptively lovely looking bush that has horrible needles, but no one is going to mess with it based on where it is. We get the best reception of any place I have ever seen in the world, it is crystal clear, it is beautiful. I should get such wonderful reception in Houston so go figure.

Everything becomes an issue, the telephone, bringing telephone lines in. Sometimes the telephone works, sometimes the telephone doesn't work. We have rather fierce weather here, and that subjects itself to all kinds of good things. Then there is the issue of the computer, ah, yes, my husband was a computer nut. He was an addict, he loved the computer, he went no place without his computer, he thought the computer was the most marvelous invention ever.

Because his original plan was to at least semi-retire and then ultimately retire and be able to work from here, it was important that he be able to be in touch with his sources. So we had the first at the time ISDN line in the entire county, certainly on our part of the peninsula. That was an interesting experience, getting that dug through the stone, brought down, connected, etc. When it works, it's terrific, for the most part, because it connects through the telephone system.

But because periodically the telephone is struck by lightning, then nothing works. It's not always terrific. I will say the fax machine, which is on it's own separate line, has been a blessing. The fax machine is reliable and keeps me in touch with the rest of the world when probably not much else is working.

So everything becomes a major issue, and everyone who comes to service you is coming from miles away, and for the most part they are very lovely about doing so. We purchased the televisions and the stereo equipment from some young men who have a shop in Waterford. Waterford is a four-hour drive from here, and these guys came after work, stayed until 10 or 11 o'clock, put the stuff together, and then, even though we invited them to stay over, got in the car, in the rain, and they toddled back to Waterford. It is a very different way of living and doing business, and much of it has a great deal to commend. We could learn a lot about all of this.

When the time came for us to actually have the furniture delivered, I had come back to Ireland about five weeks ahead of Larry. I was doing whatever I could, through pleading, through praying, through prostrating myself on the ground, whatever it took to get this house ready because the furniture, with or without our being ready, was coming. It had been shipped, it was in Cork and it was coming.

I really didn't want to not have the carpet down and all that because it was going to make things much more complicated. That was for me an experience from hell. The good news was I lost 17 pounds in those five weeks because I was: A) living in a house where you didn't have anyway to eat, that was one thing, and B) working constantly cleaning and moving and etc., etc. On Sunday, the day we were having the tile floors acid washed, which had to happen before you put other things on it, the pump decided to go, so we had no water.

Much of the time, when cleaning services would come and try to get the windows cleaned, we'd have no hot water because the timer was very temperamental. The third one seems to be fine, but the first two were very temperamental. A lack of hot water was bad enough, I was boiling on the stove constantly, but no water whatsoever? This was not a good thing.

These were some of the kinds of high-anxiety moments I had.

Then the person came to do the hardwood floor. I had already picked a specific kind of floor. You need a special kind of wooden floor when you have under-floor heating, otherwise, if it doesn't have the capacity to expand and contract properly, it will buckle. We picked the floor, the right kind of floor. I made a big, big issue of the fact that I did not want this to be a polyurethane stained floor, I wanted it to be a waxed and buffed natural floor. I get here and guess what, just guess what? It had been stained with polyurethane, and it looked awful. The wood wasn't meant for that, it's got gray streaky kind of stuff.

So I called the person and said, "This will have to come up, you'll have to strip and do whatever." This is the day the furniture is coming, I kept stressing, this is the day the furniture is coming. Oh, he'd be there in plenty of time. Well, something happened, and he wasn't there in plenty of time, and the furniture beat him, but he did come. Now, in order to strip the floor, there was a large bed that had to be moved, there was a big armoire that had to be moved. In the process of thus moving, part of the armoire crashed into the window and took down a whole wall of curtains, at which point I just stood there and said, "I'm going to lose it, I think I'm really going to lose it."

So I went upstairs and hid in one of the bedrooms and didn't speak to anybody, because I thought, I'll scream at these people and just be rude. We did get the curtains back up, we did get the painted wall that was all gouged repaired, we did get everything done. It's probably not a typical moving experience, but it's different being in another country. You have no place to just sort of go to, to get away from what you are going through when you are trying to get this house settled.

It had been a wonderful summer weather-wise until the day the movers came, and then it rained for two solid days. The movers arrived with a 40-foot container, which was required. However, there was no way that container could get down to this road, so they had to shadow it with a smaller truck. This meant that everything had to be unloaded off the container, loaded onto a small truck, brought down to our road, then unloaded again to bring into the house.

I had purchased everything that belongs in this house, unless it had an electric plug, in America. That meant all the beds, all the furniture, all the art, all the books, every cup, every saucer, every sheet, every pillow, everything was in this container. I knew how difficult it would be to find these things in Ireland. It's not that you can't find them there, but I knew it would require a lot of travel time for me every time I needed something. It was much easier to shop in a place where I knew where everything was, and still it took about a year to accumulate and put into storage all the things we needed for this house.

I had the architect give me a grid, and I worked with a woman in Houston who helped me figure out exactly what size pieces of furniture would go where. It was like playing with a dollhouse and it worked. When everything arrived and was unpacked, it worked, with a couple of exceptions. We had ordered, this is so strange, we had ordered a bed, a beautiful brass bed from a dealer in Houston. The bed was English, hence the bed came from England, went to Houston, then was crated and sent to Ireland.

Fortunately, I had the intuition to assemble everything in Houston because once it is crated and shipped it would be hard to get missing parts. Well, the connecting pieces were the wrong length, so that turned out to be just one more interesting addendum. They replaced the pieces, we assembled it, took it apart and put it in the box. What we didn't consider when we were getting the mattresses and box springs for all these beds was that American accessories are not necessarily compatible with English beds. The California-style, heavy thick stuff that we were getting for the mattress and the box springs was going to be far too thick and too high for this bed because the bed was already high off the floor.

As the movers were putting the bed together, they called me to come in and take a look at it. They had put the box spring and mattress on, and they were so high they were over the top of the bed, over the frame of the bed. I would need a ladder to get into this bed.

He said, "I think we have a problem."

"Ah, yes! Do we ever!"

These guys were so terrific, they took the mattress and the box springs off. They realized I couldn't sleep on it as it was, so they went and found a large piece of plywood , cut it to size and put the plywood on the frame. They put the mattress on the plywood, and it worked fine. It was a very nice thing for them to do because I was exhausted, and the opportunity to be able to sleep in a bed of my own after all of this moving was a most welcome opportunity to say the least. So now I have an extra California-size, queen-size box spring, and as we're unloading the others, we discover we have another extra bed frame and another extra box spring.

The garage, which isn't that big anyway, is filling up with these extra pieces of furniture, although I should say it's far better to have too much than not to have enough. The chair situation for the kitchen was requiring 10. They sent 11. That was nice because now the desk was going to have a chair without my having to go out and look for one. Some of these things turned out to be great, some of these things turned out to be a little more challenging.

Nevertheless, the opportunity to sleep here, in my own house, was wonderful, even though everything was not unpacked. I would stand at the sink because we didn't have hot water, and I would be boiling water and washing all of the dishes and all of the glasses. I think you get an adrenaline rush when you are doing this kind of a thing where you are almost compulsive. You can't stop, you've got to keep going, you've got to get it done. But it was done, and we did make it. The woman who did the "soft" furnishings was going to be coming down before my husband arrived, so she could put up the draperies and the window shades.

When Larry arrived several weeks later, we had a driver pick him up at the airport and bring him here. When he arrived, it was like something out of a Cecil B. De Mille movie. He pulls up, his driver lets him out, he comes in the house, the house is furnished, everything is in place, the curtains are up, fresh coffee is being brewed, he looks around, it's beautiful, it's wonderful and he says to me, "Well, that wasn't so bad."

It's a miracle he survived that experience alone. I didn't know whether to laugh or cry. But he thought it was beautiful. Every moment of his life here, he was so enchanted with the environment, with this house, with the people, with the place, with everything about it. And even though he never got to fully appreciate it for the long haul, what living here would mean for him, if you think in terms – and it helps me to think in these terms – of quality verses quantity, then there's no doubt this was for him really quality time. He was a person who had high energy and who had a hard time unwinding, and this was the one place that he was able to adjust to a different pace and march somewhat to a different drummer.

Someone asked us, "What do you do there?"

"You do nothing," he said, "and that's the best part of it all."

It's a place where you can actually do nothing, and you don't feel even remotely guilty about doing nothing. It's a place where you can honestly do nothing and enjoy the nothingness. I think of it as a place where I come not to do but as a place where I come to be. This place gives you the ability to get in touch with that part of yourself that, in the helter-skelter of the high-pressured life we live in most urban environments, you rarely get an opportunity to know.

It's getting in the car and driving around to the other side of the mountain and spending an afternoon with an artist whose work is just gloriously representative of what he sees when he looks out at this part of the world. This is his vista, his view of the world, a man who struggled for a very long time and now after many years has become, I guess, what you'd call a hot property. His art is selling not only in Ireland, but he has exhibitions in Colorado and in New Mexico, and he can sell his art without even going there himself. As much as he can send them, they can now sell for him.

It's going to this studio nestled in the hills of this mountain and spending an afternoon drinking tea and looking at his work and exploring his garden and having no need to be anyplace else or doing anything else that can make the living of your life a quality experience. In fairness, Larry should have had many more years of this opportunity to experience these things. He should have had time to go to a pub more often, to spend our Fridays in town where the traditional music is played on Friday nights and to drive around the mountain and visit the Zen Buddhist Monastery & Meditation Center, and to explore all of the wonderful opportunities at the music festival at the Bantry House and all of the things he didn't get enough of.

This little place in the world . . . it's a funny little spot in that I, who am a fanatic coffee drinker, can't really find a place such as Starbucks, a place where you cant go and get a decent cup of coffee. You just can't say you are going to go someplace and have a croissant and good cup of coffee, you can't do that. However, in this tiny little town, there are two crackerjack massage therapists, there is a reflexologist, there is homeopathy, there is a woman from the Netherlands who does wonderful facials and what she calls lymphatic drainage, and you can go to the Zen Meditation Center.

So it's a very funny little spot. I have a feeling, based on the folks that I have met, that many of the lost generation, the hippie generation of Europe, ended up here because they could just do their own thing. They can grow their organic vegetables and wear their Birkenstocks and do whatever, and no one would pay much attention to them. I think that accounts for a lot of the local color and the eccentricities of much of what is here.

In 2002, I think, Peter McCarthy's book, *McCarthy's Bar*, was the No. 1 best seller in Ireland. I took a proprietary interest in this book because on the cover of the book is the McCarthy's Bar that is in Castletownbere. It's our bar, it's our McCarthy's!

Peter decided he was going to visit McCarthy's Bars throughout the country. Being of Anglo-Irish ancestry, he decided he was going to find himself, his relatives and his history. He spent his summers in West Cork as a kid and was kind of retracing some of that and deciding whether or not to spend the remainder of his life permanently in Ireland or in England. I will not spoil the story for you because it is a wonderful read, it's funny, it's right on, it's spot on, as they would say here.

His description of the Beara and how wonderfully unspoiled and unlike even the nearest town, Glengarriff, is palpable. How it has an almost lush and tropical kind of environment, and how, when you go the 15 miles from Glengarriff to Castletown to the Beara, you are really in almost a moonscape looking kind of landscape. It is rocky and craggy and wild and untamed and little traveled, which is certainly the beauty of it. As a probable example of local wisdom, folks in town have opted not to do much to restore a hotel that is in a dilapidated condition right in the center of town. If you have lots of accommodations, you would have lots of tourist and lots of buses, and that is what nobody here wants. People will say, "We'll do without the money if we can just not have the invasion."

That makes being here a place where you get the sense you're living where people actually live, not where they zip through with their camcorders on a bus to have "done Ireland" in two days or less. It is a very small country, yet you barely can get from one peninsula to the next in a part of a day. When I go to Cork, which is my nearest city, we're talking a minimal three-hour drive. It is like, if I went to Austin from Houston for the day and turned around and drove back. It's doable but not the sort of thing you generally think to do.

However, if I need to go shopping or need certain services, or if I want to go to the movies, I would drive the three hours up and the three hours back in order to do that. It isn't that the distance is physically so far, it's that the kinds of roads and the meandering lanes that you have to go through, not to mention the possibility of flash flood and who knows what, make the going a lot slower than mileage would indicate.

When I am here in Ireland, when I arrive, I go into the post office and let them know I am here and how long I will be here. For that length of time, the postal carrier comes to my house and delivers the mail. If the door is open, he puts it on the counter, and it is not that he just knocks on the door and just hands it to me. I don't have a mailbox, so there really isn't any other way for him to do that. When I am not here, the local real estate person from whom we have our homeowner's insurance, keeps my mail. Just like in any little town in America probably 40 or 50 years ago this was how it was done.

Also, we now have trash collection. This is a big deal because one of the two things I was most insistent upon was a bio-cycle system, which is really a fancy septic tank that recycles. It had to be adequate to accommodate a garbage disposal because at that time there was no trash collection. You had to bag it up, put it in the car and drive it to the dump, a most unpleasant and undesirable experience. It's bad enough with trash, but we're talking now actual garbage. I do have a garbage disposal, which makes this house a one of a kind, truly.

The other thing I insisted on was an American style washer and dryer. The ones I had seen, many of the European types, heat the water in the machine. They are very tiny, so you might get only three or four towels done in two-and-a-half hours of work. When you're thinking about maybe having a house full of people who are using towels like there's no tomorrow, this was not going to work.

Often times, homes will have a 30-gallon hot water tank, but that wasn't going to cut it for me either so I had to have this big boiler that would allow us to have hot water on demand. All of these are things that are doable but not customary. They are customized, and it makes the doing of everything just that much slower.

People are curious, so folks would show up and wander down. If you drive down this road, it dead-ends at this house so you can't be going any place else if you come here. People would just kind of wander around. I would ask them if they would like to see the house, and they would definitely like to see the house. I had ample opportunity to show folks who had heard about the American house, who would want to come and take a look at it and see what are these odd things that I have.

The most fascinating to everyone truly is the side-by-side refrigerator with the icemaker and the water that comes out of the door. That is just amazing to most folks. They've never seen such a thing, and the fact that you push a button and ice cubes come out is just like a toy. It has been quite an experience.

If you want to have something dry-cleaned here, you can, but you better leave yourself lots of lead-time because it is going to take minimally a week before you get it back. Or you can go to O'Donaghue's Pub, put your dry cleaning on the 3 o'clock bus to Cork, tell them to take it to the dry cleaners, get them to put it on the next day's bus back, then you can pick it up at the pub. Only here would such a thing happen. It is just truly in many ways out of some kind of a movie. It's lovely.

Because English is spoken by most of the people in most of the country, and because one out of every four Americans claims at least some Irish background, often times Americans tend to view Ireland as a little extension of some Barry Fitzgerald movie or South Boston or Chicago. That's a mistake. This is a foreign country, and to really function well and to acclimate, one needs to bear in mind that this is not America, this is a foreign country.

As an example, during the season proceeding Lent, which is usually February, the advertisements that are running are talking about health food cereal and the benefits of eating this cereal and how good it's going to be for you. The tag line is, "Well, since you're giving up cigarettes or chocolate or meat or alcohol for Lent, be sure you take up this cereal that's going to be good for you."

I am very sensitive to advertising because I have lived in that world for a long time. That just strikes me as a hoot. In America, I cannot fathom anybody promoting something because it's commensurate with the beginning of Lent. Also, on the national radio at noon, the Angelus is played, and people stop and take their moment out for the Angelus. In the post office there is a little donation box for Little Sisters of the Poor. This is a national governmental institution. Holy days of obligation are school holidays and in some cases work holidays. The only similar experience I've ever had to this is being in Jerusalem, where the national holidays are the Jewish holidays, and where at about 3 o'clock on a Friday afternoon people leave work, shops begin to close and you shut down for the observance of the Sabbath.

That is a national, not a separate religious aspect of life. It comes across very loud and clear that this is a different place. Different is not bad, different is just different. It is an opportunity for a reflective kind of life where you can get in touch with the fact that people here live on a different plane. That's probably not a fair statement to say about people who live in Dublin, which is a very fast-paced city, or probably in the high-tech areas of Galway or Limerick.

In the rural countryside of west Cork, people live in a different place and on a different plane. It is a very good place, certainly a good place for us, and a place of hope for my husband. He was going to finally have an opportunity and time to get in sync with this lifestyle, to slow down his pace and do the things he always talked about wanting to do – to view the mountains, smell the roses, do all of those wonderful things.

Of course, the sad part for me is that he didn't live to get to do all of those things. The happy part is that, while he was here, he came as close as he probably ever came to really being able to relax and enjoy and shutdown and to experience life in a different way. There were moments when he obviously didn't do that because he was feeling a lot of financial pressure. For the most part, prior to that, he was able to really enjoy.

There is an old Bing Crosby and Ingrid Bergman movie, very corny, very hokey, very sweet, *The Bells of St. Mary's*, in which there is a song called, "The Land of New Beginnings." I am looking out at a vista that is spectacular in every aspect and thinking of this old, ancient place as truly the land of new beginnings. It was going to be a land of new beginnings for us as a couple. It now has to become that for me as an individual alone. Learning to do that is challenging to say the least.

Being here has been truly cathartic and helpful for me. It is sometimes difficult to explain why, being this far away from everything I normally know and love and this isolated from the mainstream, that would be a good or a helpful thing. Mostly, I guess, it allows me the luxury of being sad when I need to be sad, alone when I need to be alone, and to be introspective and yet have people around when I need and want to be around people.

I'm lacking the pressures of being involved in a big community, all of which are great activities and beneficial and useful and constructive, but I am allowed the luxury of not having to confront and deal with any of those.

Heartbeats:

• You can't come back until you leave. Leave the sorrow to go back to what brought you to your bliss, your joy.

• Try new things, new experiences and let yourself enjoy. The person who loved you would not want you to hurt forever.

• Be open to the kindness of strangers, it will lift your spirits and warm your heart.

• Find your "land of new beginnings," it's one of the greatest challenges of being alone but since you can't go back, going forward is the only choice.

Putting Firsts Second

CHAPTER 13

That has been a very healing kind of experience for me. I try to project into my future, which scares me because there is an aspect of one's future you can't ignore, you have to plan for and prepare for, and certainly now I have to do it in a very different way. The tenuousness of life in itself has caused me to think that the best made plans, of course, often go awry. So you live on the knife-edge of planning, being judicious and yet thinking: "I need to live in the now because the only time I have is the now, and on the memories of what was before, what was once, and the hope perhaps of what life may hold again."

I am in Ireland on Valentine's Day. We left Fort Worth last year on Valentine's Day to come here. This was the last healthy week of my husband's life. He went directly from the airport, having left here, to the hospital, never to return home again. This week, when I am here for the exact amount of time we were here last year, I am so cognizant of what came next.

It is coming up to D-day for me. I have been through the first of everything else. I have not been through the first Valentine's Day, I have not been through the first of the commemoration of my husband's death, and I have not been through those awful three weeks, which I am dreading, when he was in intensive care.

We always made a big deal out of Valentine's Day. It brought out the romantic in us. Larry always sent flowers. We bought each other gifts, usually something nice, and also something funny. We went out to dinner, we dressed up, we really celebrated. In addition to that, my husband always sent flowers to all of our daughters, subsequently our daughters-in-law and then our granddaughters. I am thinking there is a florist somewhere in Houston who is grieving over the loss of this tidy little piece of business.

All of us who looked forward to getting our flowers on Valentine's Day realized that those particular flowers will not be coming and will never be coming again. There will be no little jewelry box with a wonderful goody in it for me, perhaps ever, but certainly not in the foreseeable future and certainly not for Valentine's Day. Being here in Ireland is somewhat less painful in a sense than being in Houston because I've discovered Valentine's Day is not the same kind of big deal as it is at home.

I went in a variety of stores to try to find valentine cards to send to my grandchildren but really couldn't find anything appropriate. They're all for wives, husbands, boyfriends, girlfriends. The commercialism of the holiday hasn't gotten to the point here where they do cards for grandchildren so e-mail will have to suffice for the kids this year. Each of us in our own way and within our own family will be remembering Larry and this loss, I think, especially on this day. It was such fun to have the doorbell ring and have someone standing there with a beautiful bouquet of flowers, and you knew it was coming because he never missed a year.

This is a first again for all of us, a missing link to what had become a personal and family tradition. Each of those links forged the chain that held us together, and it's sad to think that we have lost one of those links. We have to generate new links, and we have to do it without a husband, a father, a grandfather who we all loved and loved us.

The outpouring of response to Larry's death was really quite overwhelming. Most particularly poignant was the number of cards and letters and flowers from people in Ireland, not just the people that we were particularly friends or friendly with but others as well. I would get a bouquet of flowers, and the card would say, "From your painters," and it was absolutely lovely.

Most particularly, a significant number of Mass cards came. Larry got Mass cards from several countries actually – America, Ireland, Spain and France. The man had prayers going from all directions. One might wonder about the response of somebody Jewish getting Mass cards. I thought it was lovely, and most particularly he would have just adored the whole idea. When we were in Ireland, he used to fairly regularly go to Mass with one of our friends. This is a man who might have been, at least, he was a self-described closet Catholic. He used to say, "I would be a great Catholic."

But he was who he was, and he certainly had no intentions of becoming anything else. He has been to a consecration of a bishop in Houston, at the invitation of the bishop. He had been at the ordination of a priest in New Orleans at no one's invitation, he just crashed it, and he was a regular or a fairly regular attendee at Mass in Ireland. He never missed a chance in New York, never at least when I was with him, to drop in and pay a visit to St. Patrick's Cathedral. He would ask me, "What does this mean?" or "Translate this for me."

I asked him when he went to Mass in Ireland what it was about it he particularly liked because what appealed to me in the old days was what I call the bells and the smells. I liked the incense and the bells that would be rung at the consecration and the chanting of the Latin like a mantra. It's probably why Hebrew Trope as a prayer language appeals to me so because I think a separate language from your everyday vernacular language as a language for prayer transports one into another realm of reality and I like that. He said he liked to go because he liked the propriety. The people were quiet, he liked that, and he liked the fact that people knelt. He thought a little humility didn't hurt anybody, but best of all he liked the fact that you were in and out, sermon, service, the whole nine yards, in 25 minutes. He thought that was, for sure, the greatest thing since sliced bread, that all services should be this short.

I am not sure how much you get done in 25 minutes or how much of an atmosphere you even get to create in 25 minutes, but he thought that was the best. He would infrequently go up the road and pop in at Sunday Mass. I've wondered what people must have thought because I have a strong feeling most of the people in this part of the country have never met anybody Jewish and don't really understand that it's not sort of an offbeat Christian sect. I think there are now less than two thousand Jews in the whole country, almost all of whom are in Dublin along with a smattering in Cork.

The chance of anyone running into someone Jewish or having any knowledge of Jewish ritual and/or the Jewish belief system or tradition is somewhere in the neighborhood of slim and none. So what they must have thought about him showing up at Mass I couldn't say. I can say, however, that I would loved to have been a fly on the wall when that discussion took place.

For me, being in Ireland much of the time means that I need to create my own Jewish aura, my own Jewish experience here. Partly that's not so difficult because in Judaism most of what is celebratory takes place at home. That's the upside. The downside is that Judaism is a communal or corporate religion far more than an individualistic one, therefore you need a community with whom to experience your Jewishness. That for me is more than slightly difficult.

However, what I do do, and have done since I have been here, is have a Shabbat dinner. Often time, I invite people to share my Shabbat dinner and explain to them exactly what I'm doing. It's a learning experience for all of us because I found that, no matter how much I teach, the best way to learn anything is to teach someone else.

I light Shabbat candles, I have a beautiful filigree menorah we purchased for a gift for this house when we were in New Orleans celebrating our last wedding anniversary, and so it has great significance. When you turn it over, it has two receptacles for Shabbat candles, and on the opposite side it has eight lovely receptacles for Hanukkah menorah. We have here a Waterford Kiddush cup with Hebrew letters on it, which I use for Friday night, and I have even taken to making my own challah because there is no way I can buy it here.

I realize how spoiled I am when there are any number of bakeries I can go to in Houston, including even a supermarket, and pick up a kosher challah for Friday with no strain or pain verses taking several hours to make it from scratch. It, however, is a tactile experience and a reminder of who I am and what I am doing and why I am baking this bread; it isn't just simply bread, it is the bread that we use for Shabbat.

The lighting of candles in Jewish tradition, which is the welcoming in of Shabbat, has been traditionally a deed that has been the prerogative of women. It is a very powerful symbol and is the calling in of the Shekinah, which is representative of the female spirit of God. In the total completion and perfection of the universe, the female spirit and the male spirit of the God head will be unified, but it is the calling of the Shekinah into your presence that is done by women at Shabbat when they do the blessing of the candles.

There are many other reasons why people light candles but this particular one has a great appeal to me. It is also interesting to me to note that the spirit of compassion, of kindness is *rachmones* and the root word, *ruah* comes from the word womb. That is also a word of female orientation, and *rachmones* or compassion or kindness or caring is a very big concept in Jewish life.

It appeals to me that these are concepts that are part of my gender's contribution, the ability to connect that with where I am, here in this land of spirit and water and stone and fire. Interestingly enough in the Irish lore the fire is never to be let out, much like the eternal flame, I guess, in a synagogue, but one never lets one's hearth fire go out.

That is the obligation or the responsibility or the privilege of the woman of the house, and there is a special ancient Celtic blessing that precedes Christianity and goes with that experience. I am finding these connections, these very old and ancient connections, to be very meaningful. The longer I live here, the more opportunity I have, I hope, to explore them. In Jewish tradition, one would use water as a spiritually purifying element.

Certainly water and sacred wells were a very big Druidic Celtic ancient tradition and experience, and they're still around. One can go to, and many people do make pilgrimages, to the old sacred wells. I guess it is the equivalent in some respects to people going to Lourdes and people collecting holy water because they feel it is sacred in healing properties.

In this remote and wonderful magical part of the world, there are many things that one is unable to easily purchase. They aren't needed here, they aren't used here, they're not known here, and they mostly are not available here. However, going into my local Supervalu is a true gift from the gods because in this place you actually can get all kinds of odd and unusual things as well as the everyday kinds of things.

I was making a trip into town and one of the things on my grocery list was asparagus. I had been to Cork the previous weekend and had noticed in the markets there that they had fresh asparagus. I was having folks for dinner and thought this would be a nice thing to serve. There was no asparagus, it hadn't been ordered and wasn't available, end of discussion.

As I was going up and down the aisles, I noticed in these sort of health foods or exotic food sections that they had a box of Rakusen's matzos. I absolutely stopped dead in my tracks. In Houston we had to find a distributor in Dallas and have these matzos ordered from the distributor and sent to our office in Houston. They are English and have a very nice flavor, a crispy kind of quality to them.

To find a box of Rakusen's matzos on the shelf in the Supervalu in Castletownbere just blew my mind. Of all of the odd and unusual things, who would have ordered it, who would have even bought it or eaten it, is simply amazing to me. This place never fails to astonish me. On this particular trip into town, it was a very pretty day after weeks of rain and wind and dreariness. I noticed that many of the people en route had their doors open. When I speak about people having their doors open, I don't mean simply that they were unlocked, I mean the front door is wide open.

This is presumably to air out the house and let a little fresh air and sunshine in. I am trying to remember the last time in America when one would feel safe just literally opening and leaving open the front door of the house let alone make it available to any and all who chose to come and wander in.

There is a practice here that I refer to as an economy of motion. It only happens in the country, it would not be a city gesture. It probably only happens in this part of the country. As you are driving along the road, it's imperative that you keep both hands on the wheel because the roads are, to say the least, a challenge. As you are driving along the road, when you pass another car, you don't wave, you don't give that teeth-baring grin that is so typically American. You raise one finger, your index finger, you salute with one finger. You and the person approaching salute each other with the raising of the one finger off the steering wheel.

This is such a localized experience. The only place I have ever seen anything at all comparable is when I was a very young college-age woman and had the chance to drive around in a sports car for a while. Sports car drivers would do that, they would pass each other and give this abbreviated salute in recognition.

This is the way drivers acknowledge one another, particularly if you've had to pull over or stop or slow down in order to let somebody else pass. It is your way of acknowledgment. In Texas we would raise our hand and wave at somebody who would let us into traffic. In Ireland, this is accomplished with one finger, it is a true economy of motion.

Also, we discovered that people who sit at table for a very long time, including those with young children, which is fascinating to me, tend to lean into one another. It's what they call huddling and has a very practical aspect. In a village or a town or a country where there are no secrets, if you want to have any kind of a discussion and not include the entire room, you lean in and speak softly to the people who are at your immediate table. It was such fun for me to be someplace where people speak softly because so often people will say, "I can't hear you Suzanne, speak up Suzanne." Now I am in a country where everybody talks softly, and I'm the one that is not the odd man out. This was pure pleasure.

Many, many years ago, Larry and I had the unique opportunity to become friends with the great, late Paul O'Dwyer, who was the Irish American civil rights litigator of note of the 20th century. He had come as a young man to America, worked on the docks, put himself through law school, practiced law as an adult at 99 Wall Street, overlooking the Brooklyn docks where he had landed as a kid because he said he never wanted to forget where he came from.

His brother, William O'Dwyer, was the ill-fated mayor of New York. Paul was the person remembered for all of his great contributions to American civil liberties. He was a partner in a law firm known as O'Dwyer and Bernstein. They had a practice whereby one of them would take six months and do pro bono work.

For example, Paul had spent time with the coal miners to help secure their rights, and the other partner stayed in New York to generate the revenue that would support the pro bono work. I happened to have the occasion to meet him because the congregation to which we belong in Houston some years ago had a series of contemporary moral issues, one of them being the issue of Northern Ireland. Paul was invited to come and speak and address the issue as he saw it from his perspective.

It fell, to my great good fortune, to me to be the person to pick him up and bring him from the airport to the hotel, during the course of which I got to know him, and we established rapport and liked one another. He said to me, "When you come to New York, be sure and call," which we did on more than one occasion. He used to send to me in Houston the Jewish publication from Ireland known as *The Yiddish Sons of Erin*. If that didn't just absolutely break me up to every now and again get this wonderful package from O'Dwyer. Of course, I was not yet aware what an extraordinary and famous person he really was.

When you walked down a street in Manhattan with Paul O'Dwyer, everyone, and I mean everyone, stopped and said, "Good day, Mr. O'Dwyer, good morning Mr. O'Dwyer, nice to see you Mr. O'Dwyer." He was a man of moderate height. When I knew him, he was minimally in his 70's, still having incredible energy, still practicing. He had steel blue eyes and a shock of white hair. When he looked at you and meant business, you knew he really did mean business.

Getting to know Paul O'Dwyer was a great, great treat. One time when we went for coffee with him after spending a little time in his office, he and I and Larry were all talking, but he and I were talking in the tone of voice that we were accustomed to talking in. Larry kept saying, "Pardon me, I can't hear you." I was in hog heaven. Here I was talking to somebody who actually could hear me, who spoke in the same tone of voice I did. This was really, really a pleasure.

A true and darling story about Paul O'Dwyer was one that took place once when we were in New York in October. My husband was going to go to a meeting in Brooklyn, and I had truly no desire to go to Brooklyn. I decided that, since I rode, I was going to go to Central Park. I was going to rent a horse and ride around for the day. At that time they no longer had horses available in Central Park. You had to go to Claremont Stables on West 86th Street. The woman was very nice, she made a phone call and told them I was coming, and they would have the horse tacked and ready to ride.

Mind you, I am doing this in a cashmere sweater and pearls because I hadn't really come prepared to ride, but the weather was just too perfect to resist. I took a cab over to the Claremont Stables and got on my horse with the little map they'd given me describing how to get to the park, how to ride around the bridal path and how to get back. I don't do maps really very well. I can usually get someplace okay, but I don't usually have the best sense of direction when it comes to reversing myself and getting back. However, I figured the horse had done this a million times and would know where we were going.

I think this horse had been in the barn just a little too long because he was very spirited and very anxious to get going. We are trotting along in the park, moving along at a nice clip, when all of a sudden this horse dashes out of the park. We are now not on a bridle trail, we are on one of the Manhattan busy streets. The horse is now just going where he chooses to go. The map is useless to me, I have no idea not only where I am but how I am going to get from where I am back to where I need to be. In the course of this adventure, I ended up on Amsterdam Avenue at which there were, I think, six intersecting signals. People are honking, taxis are honking, and I am scared the horse is going to spook and throw me. However, I figured eventually given his head, this horse will go home.

Next he led me through a neighborhood that I think was predominantly Puerto Rican. People brought their children out on the stoop to wave. I waved and felt like a queen, riding on this horse through this neighborhood waving at people. Two-and-a-half hours later, the horse did finally make its way back to the Claremont Stables. The people there, of course, were very nervous. They wanted to know where I was. They wanted to know what had happened to their horse. I gave them the short version, took my purse, went back to the hotel, took a quick shower, then took a cab to O'Dwyer's because I was suppose to meet with Larry and Paul there at 4 o'clock.

When I arrived, Paul asked me what I had done that day.

I said, "Well, as luck would have it, I took this horse for a ride and had this adventure."

He, with this wonderful twinkle in his eyes, said, "Oh, darling, I'm so happy to hear you used a horse from Claremont Stables, it's the last stable we have in Manhattan."

I said, "Really, I wasn't aware of that."

He said, "Yes, awhile ago we were having this major city discussion at the city council about whether or not we should keep the stables. One of my colleagues kept saying, 'It's a health hazard, it's a pollutant and we need to get rid of the stables.'"

I kept saying, "But it is the only stables left, and people want to ride around the bridle path."

Finally, in desperation and in answer to one of his colleagues, who I think was an African American council member, Paul O'Dwyer said to him in his own unique and amicable way, "It would seem to me, my friend, that there are a few more serious problems than a little horse shit on West 86th Street."

At which point the issue was shelved, and the Claremont Stables lived to thrive another day. That was one of my wonderful experiences with Paul O'Dwyer, the great, famous Irishman who had this delightful, soft-spoken manner about him but who had been on the charge for almost all of the great social movements and political movements in American life in the latter part of the 20th century. He was a font of information of history and of social action and of causes, some of which he won, some of which he lost. To his very dying day, he never gave up the fight.

He had been on more than one occasion the Grand Marshall for the St. Patrick's Day Parade in New York City, however, in the later part of his life he refused to participate because he was in protest against the prohibition of gays and lesbians. That was Paul O'Dwyer, that was typical of the kinds of things he did. He represented people legally who probably could have never afforded the kind of legal representation he provided, and he did it out of a sense of cause and a sense of social responsibility. It was a great pleasure and a great honor in my life to have known him.

I think of him often when I am here because in County Mayo, where he came from, he founded a home for kids who are orphaned or are in need of some sort of rehabilitation. It was always a great honor for us to contribute to his home and to his cause, considering how many things he did for the rest of us.

In the Irish house, we have only Irish art, which seems appropriate. Most of it we purchased in Dublin and a couple of pieces in Limerick. One was a wonderful sculpture that was a gift of an artist friend, and one piece is from a local. While in Dublin, Larry used to like to hang out in this particular gallery and visit with the guys there to "schmooz" as it is called. He would negotiate, he loved the process of negotiating. There was at that time a living artist named Markey Robinson, who was renowned at the time and whose work was very pricey. We could never afford to buy his things while he was alive, and when he died shortly thereafter, of course, his pieces became even more valuable.

He was a most eccentric old man, old even at the time we met him. He had traveled around the world in a tramp steamer and had, to say the least, a colorful life. Even as an old man, he liked to find someone to tell his stories to and to listen to him, and he most of all liked to find some gullible woman. Because I was a captive audience, I became his gullible woman, or at least I became his audience. He would show up very regularly when he knew we were going to be there because here was someone who hadn't heard all of his stories and would be polite enough to listen.

At one point he proceeded to tell me that I was what he considered a "plausible woman". Where but in Ireland would somebody call you a plausible woman? This was a compliment, I am not sure exactly what it meant, but it was a compliment. I think I was a plausible woman because I was willing to listen to the most important topic of conversation in his universe, which was himself. Use of language here is musical and lyrical and flowery and descriptive, and Mr. Robinson used all of these terms to apply to himself. Because I would listen to his stories, some of which were extremely far-fetched, I was in his estimation, a plausible woman. Not a lovely woman, not a kind woman, not an attractive woman, a plausible woman.

As an example of the use of language, I chose to check out what people use for valentine greetings, the kinds of things we all find in newspapers throughout the world where people have a heart or a poem, etc. Here is a valentine heart in the classifieds, and this is what it says, "Alice, before you get up, take an independent look under the pillow, it will open your eyes." I dare you to find anyplace in the world where that message would be considered a valentine message.

It was certainly good for me to find something to be able to chuckle about on Valentine's Day because this, of course, is a day for lovers. Valentine's Day for me is particularly sad. It is not only the last time of a memory of a valentine, but I am now getting into the countdown of the numbers of days that I can say, "Last year at this time we did this." Pretty soon that year will be gone, and I won't be able to even have the immediacy of feeling, "This is what we did last year at this time." In this case, last year we were on our way to Ireland, where I spent what was to be the last healthy week of my husband's life.

It is so poignant and so full of every mixture of emotion, good and bad. I don't know where I would have been any happier because I don't think this is a week I would be happy at any place. I don't think being in Houston, where all of the reminders of places we had frequented in the past for Valentine's Day, would have been so up-front and center, would have been any more comforting. Being where we were, where he was, and where he was at his happiest, offers a sense of connection, of bringing his presence into my life at this time. I am counting down to the days now when I will be leaving here on the very exact day we left last year. I will be flying the same flight, same route, only this time I will be alone.

I will not be going to the hospital as I had to do last time. I will be in the countdown of the commemorative year. I'll be facing the unveiling of his tombstone, the actual yaartzeit, the anniversary of the commemoration of his death. I will have gone through one full year of all of the rituals, of all of the holidays, of all of the personal and private experiences we shared. I will have been through all of this one time.

I had thought it would be a relief to be at this point but now I'm not really sure this is necessarily true. What I am finding is that being here in Ireland for this time is catharsis for me. Frankly, the person I need to worry about now and take care of is me. Grieving, I'm finding, doesn't proceed on sort of an incline, where it gets a little better every day. It's not an incrementally improved situation, it seems to eddy like water in a current, it seems to flow a little bit smoother some days, a little rougher other days. It is not predictable. I realized I was going to have some tough moments at this season of the year, and I realized I was going to be lonely and sad, but I didn't realize the depth of that and the finality of it.

I truly thought I had come to grips with the finality of death and probably, by and large, I have, but because it's Valentine's Day, I still kept waiting for the doorbell to ring and the flowers to arrive. That's in defiance of all that is sane and sensible. It is obvious that grieving doesn't have a calendar time frame. Grieving is not defined by days on a calendar, grieving is something that comes and goes, and ebbs and flows, and gets less painful, for the most part but then will suddenly cause a jab of memory that is a fresh wound all over again.

I don't know how long that will continue. I can say in candor that it is less painful on a day-to-day basis than it was a month ago or certainly six months ago. I am less fearful of my future and my situation than I was six months ago. I take no solace in the fact that living on a fixed income and looking at what happens to the American stock market, even the bond market, doesn't make a person feel safe, sound and secure, but you can tighten your belt and you can do a lot to minimize expenses. I am blessed to have many resources to draw from in order to live a very good life and to care for myself in a way that allows me to experience most of the good things of life.

I have access to healthcare, I have the ability to travel, I have a fabulous home in Ireland, a wonderful place to live in Houston, I have no outstanding debt, I have a great family, and I am blessed with a keen mind and an incurable and insatiable curiosity. All of those are the pluses and the good things. But as everyone who has lost a loved one knows, no matter how good the things are, no matter how great life is, if you haven't the ability to share it with the person you love the most in the world, it loses a lot of its luster.

The first round of grief that really puts you into a state of shock, a denial mode, a robot state almost, is over. Now I need to find not just the courage and the energy to get out of bed and get going every day, now I need to find the reason, the raison 'd' etre for myself to do those things. How am I going to live the rest of my life? What is going to give meaning to the rest of my life? What am I going to have to look forward to? Not just going here, or doing this, but what is going to give me the sense of satisfaction and accomplishment and shared experience for the whole rest of my life?

I don't have any idea of knowing how long that will be but just being able to project ahead, which is never a smart thing to do, I guess, is a good step. So is being able to say, "Gee, five years from now, am I still going to be doing all these things basically by myself and is that going to be okay for me?" In many ways, it's very much okay for me now because I don't want to have to be involved with, connected to, accountable to, or share with another adult at this point. I am not in any way, shape or form ready to do that. I may never be ready to do that or may never have the desire and/or the opportunity to do that. I feel very married, which seems so strange to me. It is like having a husband who has gone AWOL or something.

He's gone, he's not coming back, I know that, but I still feel very married. I feel like I am not just myself, Suzanne, not just the mother of children. I truly feel that I am Larry's wife. I haven't reached the point in my own head where I am Larry's widow. Maybe that will come, I assume with time it will, but in this year it has not. I feel very much a married person. I think about him as I would think about him if he were alive, about how I'm going to share this with him, and how I'm going to tell him about that, and wait until he hears about this, and wait until he sees that, and wait till he gets home, etc., etc. The operative part of that thinking is the "wait until," and I can wait and wait and wait until hell freezes over, and there isn't going to be a coming home, a sharing, a phone call, an anything.

In my head, I know that. In my heart I really know that also, but something in my subconscious has not yet been willing or able to let go of the aura, the presence, the immediacy of my husband. I still have the feeling I am very much married. This may well be a protective device that keeps me from being more frightened or more isolated than I might otherwise feel, and that is fine. It might be transient, and that's fine too. It certainly was a real operative in my life almost one year out from my being widowed.

It may be a good thing to mention that there are, as we all know who have lost somebody, as many ways to grieve as there are people who are grieving. What works for one person doesn't necessarily work for somebody else. Therefore, to put must, ought, should rules around grieving is a total injustice to the people who are undergoing the experience. It is fallacious and doesn't work.

However, there are certain things that probably all of us should red flag and be aware of, specifically, things that are not under the umbrella of normal. These are things we should talk to somebody about and include:

1. If after several months you're still not sleeping;
2. If you're still not eating;
3. If you're eating constantly;
4. If you're drinking more than is healthy;
5. If you've lost interest in all outside activity, in all friends, in all family;
6. If you cry more than you laugh six or eight months down the road;
7. If you are truly unable to take those first halting steps at doing what you need to do to protect your own interest;
8. If you feel life is not worth living and you think, ever, about ending your own life.

If any of this fits your list, run, don't walk to the nearest grief counseling person, to the nearest mental health professional. There are people who can help you, people who know what the experience is like, people who can meet you psychologically and help you get from here to there, people who can assist you in defining your own goals in ways that may help you reach them. There are people who can hold your hand if that's what you need, who can allow you to unload your anger because that has to go someplace, and people who will let you express your sadness, your fear, your anxiety, your hurt, your disappointment, your abandonment, your rejection, your anger. All of those things, none of which are positive, happy moments, a professional can allow you to voice, to vent, and help you work through them. There are times when a good friend may be able to do a whole lot of that also. Good friends will have their own issues with you and their own concerns about you and their own emotional attachment to you in ways that somebody who is a pro will not.

I cannot stress strongly enough that, if you are a person experiencing grief, have any doubts about where you are in this, or even if you just feel you need some validation and a hand to hold, you should seek professional help. For some, a group experience might make you more comfortable. There are grief counseling groups where people learn from the experience and benefit from the experiences of others, some of whom are maybe six or eight months or a year or two further along than you. They can say, "Oh yes, at this time this is where I was, but now I'm here."

By example, that is hopeful and optimistic. I deal with my things my way as does everyone else. I come from very strong stock. It's just the way it is. It has been very enabling and empowering for me to be able to rely on that. It isn't a weakness to need to seek help and assistance. I have done it from the very beginning of my husband's death. I actually was sitting in the limousine behind the hearse waiting to go to the cemetery when a friend of mind who is a grief counselor poked her head in just to say, "I love you, and I care about you."

I said to her, "I am coming to see you as soon as I can." I have done that, and she has been a great help to me because I can tell her things and I can work through things with her that I wouldn't be able to work through alone. I wouldn't be able to work through them with one of my own friends or my own family either.

Remember, this is the kind of loss I had never experienced. I have two living parents, so I have never buried anybody that close to me before. Certainly there were grandparents and aunts and uncles but these were very old people whose time in life had come, and it was expected, it was following long-term illnesses.

In some cases, for those people, death was a gift, a release from pain and suffering and no hope of recovery. They had lived long, full lives. None of this was operative in my husband's case, so what I felt was robbed, cheated, left, rejected, abandoned, angered, floundering, alone, none of which is on anybody's hit parade of top 10 best feelings.

What I have learned is that each of us has a reservoir of strength and resources we probably are unaware of until it has been seriously tested and that help is available. People really do care, and you can do more than you ever thought you could do because now you must. Necessity is truly the mother of invention.

The can-do attitude is only possible once the inevitable sense of depression has begun to lift. If it doesn't lift, then by all means, get help. There are times when people need pharmaceutical assistance, they need to take medication. Maybe not forever but certainly for a while.

If your doctor thinks professional help is important for you, than I think you should definitely consider that. I'm leery of long-term drug taking because I am frankly scared of drug taking. That's my thing, it doesn't mean that it doesn't work for other people and that it isn't necessary. After all, every day of my life I take things for my osteoporosis, and it never worries me that I am going to get addicted to osteoporosis medication, so it is a question of what is medically required or desirable for you as the recovering person.

The person who died is no longer suffering, is no longer coping, is no longer dealing. But the survivor is, and how you survive and how you cope will have a great deal to do with how you can build the rest of your life. Lots of times the desire to go on with your life or to build a new life is just not there, it's nonexistent, it's "Who gives a damn?"

I'm being a brave person by simply getting up and putting one foot in front of the other and paying my bills and doing minimal things. For a while, that's absolutely true. You should get a gold medal for just doing minimal things because it requires an inordinate effort and energy just to do the bare minimum.

That does tend to pass a little. When Larry died, and we were talking to the grandchildren about what this was all about, we explained that normally people go to the hospital, they get better and they come home. This time, however, you have a grandparent who went into a hospital but did not get better, did not come home. These are kids some of whom themselves have had to go into the hospital. So the whole concept is very scary for them. Since children are extraordinarily egocentric, they naturally will ask, "Okay, if I have to go to the hospital, am I never going to come out, or is this going to happen now to my mother or my father or my grandmother?" So a lot of reassuring was needed. That also has to come from both the parents and the grandparents of any small children.

We have a set of identical twins, Alex and Arielle, in our family, and they asked me about three or four days into Shivah, "How are you doing? How do you feel?" I thought I really owed them, as best I can, an honest answer to this question. I don't think it would have been sufficient to say, "I'm doing fine," or "I'm going to be okay." I tried to think in terms of what would be meaningful to eight-year-olds. I said, "I guess what I feel like is when you are running and you fall and skin your knee and it hurts a lot and it bleeds a lot.

After a little while, it begins to form a scab, a scab sometimes comes up and oozes stuff and it still hurts when you bend your knee but it doesn't hurt as bad as it did when you first fell down. Soon, from the inside out, you get new skin, and it grows and the scab falls off. Now when you bend your knee, it doesn't hurt any more but for as long as you live the scar is always there."

This is how I think I feel. From the inside out, I will get better and I will heal but always, always the scar will be there. Even though it will hurt less, the scar will always be there. This is an experience children can relate to, one they have lived, one that makes some sense to them. We found that developing little stories or little rituals or little analogies that are appropriate for children was very beneficial and very helpful to them. It also was very beneficial and very helpful to me because now I have to verbalize what it is I'm actually feeling in a way that is age-appropriate.

That is, again, a healing healthy experience for me. It's my way of saying to all who are undergoing this experience, "Don't be afraid to talk about it, even to children, because they are frightened, they are unsettled and they will need to know." Also don't forget that because their attention span isn't too fabulous, they will need to be reassured over and over and over again.

I had an experience with my then four-and-a-half-year-old grandson, Harrison, who began to avoid me like the plague. I noticed that he was very standoffish with me, and he had not been that way before. One day I was asked by his mom to pick him up at school. I said, "sure." He was running into the principal's office where I was to pick him up. When he looked at me, he didn't say hi! He didn't say anything. He just looked at me and said, "Why did Pepa die?" I knew that this little kid had been holding this fear of, "I don't want to get close to her because she is going to die and leave me also."

This was my chance. He had asked me that question so this was my chance to talk to him about why people die and why some things in life don't have any answers, why there are questions we don't have any answers for. He needed to know that I wasn't going to die and that I wasn't going to leave him and that I could hug him and it was okay. Children have various ways of expressing their grief.

We gave each of the children who was old enough to be at the funeral something of Larry's that they were to hold, they could fondle it and hold it and it was his, maybe it was a handkerchief, maybe it was a comb, he collected little odds and ends of things that are called chotchkes. He had a lot of little goodies and everybody had one. Nicholle said she took hers with her to bed at night so she could hold on to this thing she had that was from her grandfather, and often times she cried at night alone in her bed because she felt so bad about losing her grandfather.

Fortunately, we had some quality time when we could talk about this. We tend to think because children don't manifest any kind of obvious grieving all the time like adults do that it's not going on within them. But it is, and you have to explain the facts of life to kids over and over and over again. When a kid five years old says, "Where did I come from?" and you give him the whole long story and he looks at you and says, "Well I just wanted to know. Johnny came from Chicago, where did I come from?"

You can overkill the subject greatly, but small children need to be reinforced over and over again. The whole topic of death and the whole ability to talk about death and the sadness and the loss and the grieving are important because they don't have the emotional equipment and the experience to handle something that traumatic.

Most of the adults in their lives aren't going to have that experience or equipment either but hopefully will be better prepared than small children would be. It is imperative that small children not be left out of the loop when we have conversations about death. In my family, it would have been *verboten*, nobody would have ever talked about somebody being dead in front of a child. That only enhances a child's fear. Where did they go? What happened to them? Will this happen to me, will this happen to my mother? I know I have feelings about this, but nobody is addressing them, nobody is talking about them so they must be bad. That is something you don't want to have happen to the children who are experiencing the fallout from the loss of someone who meant a great deal to them and whom they loved deeply.

One might have thought, certainly I might have thought, that the fact that I spent most of my advanced academic life and a great deal of my adult life dealing in a serious, systematic, scholarly way with the big questions of life, the meaning of life and death, morality, mortality, truth, goodness, justice, a sense of ethics, a sense of transcendence, an understanding of what symbols mean, combined with a prayer life and a community life and ritual, would have been exceedingly helpful to me during this year. Unfortunately, I must say in all candor it has not. I have had the wonderful opportunity to study with many enlightened, instructive, insightful, intuitive people in my life. At one point, I was the area director in Houston for the American Jewish Committee. During that time, I had a rare and wonderful opportunity to study for a while as part of a consortium of Jews and Christians in America at an event sponsored by the Jewish Theological Seminary and the Auburn Theological Seminary. The conversation was scintillating, it was enlightening, it was a memorable event, something I will always treasure having experienced.

Two particular folks made a great impression upon me, two particular scholars. One was Professor Shaye Cohen, who at the time was with the Jewish Theological Seminary and is a foremost scholar on New Testament scripture. The other is Rabbi Irving Greenberg, who is a pioneer and a true enlightened soul, not only in American Jewish thought but in world Jewish thought. It was at this particular symposia that I heard Rabbi Greenberg discuss the possibility of exploring what Jews and Judaism might learn from our Christian neighbors about the concept of grace and how that may be applicable in Jewish terms.

This is really heavy stuff, and I was just delighted to hear the kinds of discussions and conversations he had. Having just finished Harvey Cox, the Harvard theologian's book, *Common Prayers*, I came across a quote Cox uses of Rabbi Greenberg's in which he says,

"Human beings cannot be mature until they encompass a sense of their own mortality. To recognize the brevity of human existence gives urgency and significance to the totality of life. To confront death without being overwhelmed, driven to evasions or dulling of the senses is to be given life again as a daily gift."

This is probably the most helpful thing I have encountered this entire year. What I found has worked for me has been very surprising. Actually, it's a return to the very elements of not only life but of creation. I can return to this wonderful home in Ireland, this stone home that sits on a ledge of stone, and feel as if I have been harbored in my cave. I am almost in a womb.

I take care of this house but, conversely, this house protects me and looks after me. I can be in touch with the silence, the pure lovely silence that allows me to experience my own feelings, my own emotions, my own sensations or the lack of them. I can feel the wind on my face and hear it rushing through the trees; I can smell the air coming off the sea; I can walk the craggy land and be truly, literally grounded in the only way that at this point is making any sense to me; I can feel the clay of my being responding to the clay of being, and that has been very powerful for me. It has allowed me on the very simplest of levels to feel somehow still connected to life. It has been the elemental forces and the elemental aspects of creation that has allowed me to do this.

When I now hear the expression, "ashes to ashes and dust to dust," it has a whole different meaning for me. It no longer means or resonates with the concept of death and decay, it means to me that a return to the earth is going to enable life to once again take place, the inner life of the soul. It is the winter of my soul, it is the autumn of my life looking at things in a seasonal cyclical way. If I am ever to experience a springtime of the soul, it will be because I am doing the hibernating I need to do. I am doing it in this very elemental way that has allowed me to become in touch with the things that are so primal and so necessary and without which life on the planet is not sustainable. These are the things that have allowed some glimmer of new life to focus in me.

I came across an article in the *Wall Street Journal* a few months ago written by Merle Rubin who wrote about clichés. I loved it because I had written a bit in this book about how I did not wish to speak in clichés or, God forbid, become one. She had this wonderful column about clichés being lots of talk and lots of nonsense. She talked about the constantly bantered- about term of closure, how one is suppose to get "closure" on one's grief. She pointed out that closure probably works at the end of a book and probably works well at the end of a musical piece, but it doesn't work that way with human experiences. In a personal life, you don't get the same kind of closure, so now we close the book and we turn the page and we move on.

It certainly doesn't seem to be that way with something as serious as the loss of a spouse or, I presume, the loss of a child or any other person that one loves deeply. She also tackles the concept of, "I'll always be there for you." Usually, people say that as they're sort of drifting out the door. The "I'll always be there for you," is another form of psychobabble for which I have developed little or no appreciation.

Also, she talks about the concept of, "Deal with it." How one deals with it, whatever the "it" is, is certainly a highly individualistic and a highly personal technique one develops, I think, by hit or miss or by trial or error, but it is very painful and it is done step by step. When people say to a grieving person, "You just have to deal with it," it's generally said because they are not the ones having to "deal with it." She goes on to say that for centuries we somehow managed to get along well enough without all of these gems and that she was somehow going to muddle through and get along without them in the future.

Her overall take on the triteness of clichés is that it is a means of using psychobabble to avoid having to, "deal with," as she would say, the difficult and painful things that we all have to go through in life. There are probably appropriate words and appropriate terms for these, but the current list of trite clichés is not in that lexicon.

Earlier, I mentioned how I was working at combining my Jewishness with an absolutely Catholic environment, devoid of any kind of Jewish content, so I am reaching for areas of similarity. One of the things of definite similarity is that both Judaism and Celtic tradition have a blessing for almost everything. In Ireland they also have a toast for almost everything. In many cases, I think they are probably interchangeable. To jump back to Pete McCarthy's No. 1 best seller in Ireland, *McCarthy's Bar*, the author found a quote in a guidebook that is an Irish blessing bestowed upon anyone who reads it. He found it very charming, and I do, too. It was in the inscription in a guidebook that reads,

"A blessing on all who read this book".

I would wish it for anyone who has had the graciousness to read this book and who is dealing with any of the hard issues life tends to afford you when you have suffered the loss of someone you love.

I am living at the moment of countdown time, similar to the expectation you have when you are watching a launch for NASA. In a few days, I shall be leaving Ireland on the exact same day Larry and I left Ireland and this home that he loved so dearly last year. He never went home, he went directly from the airport to the hospital, where after three-and-a-half weeks of intensive care and an unsuccessful heart surgery, he finally died. I'm measuring these days and savoring these days because never again will there be a time, using time as a reference, when I can say, even to myself, last year at this time we were here, last year at this time we did this.

I can say two years from now or three years from now, but somehow that first year has become sacred time for me, probably because you mark anniversaries on an annual calendar. Also, I have become in my own healing, so cyclically oriented to the concept of the time and the turning of the wheel of the time that will soon bring me face to face with the surgery that didn't work, the coma that only deepened, the realization that he was not ever going to recover due to severe brain damage, and finally the ultimate letting go and allowing him to be free of the fetters that were binding his soul and his spirit to a body that could no longer service him.

The rainbow has come to represent everything from the covenantal relationship in the Bible between God and Noah to the rainbow connection of Kermit the Frog. Ireland is a place where it rains frequently, often times very softly while the sun is still shinning. Such a day is referred to as a soft day, and there are frequent and spectacular rainbows.

They have an appeal to almost everyone, of course, and a special appeal to me because, on our very last drive from our Irish house to the airport to return to Houston, the mountain pass was just flooded with rainbows. They would split the mountains, and the spectrum of light, color and beauty was just overwhelming. We stopped frequently along the way and took many pictures. It was of great delight and great pleasure to Larry, who, even though he wasn't feeling well at the time, just couldn't resist the opportunity to stop and look and take pictures.

I tried to think about the rainbow as a smile of nature, maybe even a kiss of nature, and to fix that in my memory and in my mind's eye. That's because some of what I'd faced at the end of that first year required all of the warmth and comforting thoughts I could call forth. First of all, I had to, earlier in the year, go to a monument place and select the gravestone for my husband.

Traditionally, the grave does not have a stone in Jewish lore until close to a year after the passing of someone. Stone monument places are not warm and inviting. They are grimy and messy and very gritty and business like. So here I was, picking out a piece of black granite and deciding what I would have etched on my husband's gravestone. Black and gray were his favorite choices for any kind of logo, so I definitely had the chiseling done in gray.

It is a very simple site, it had his name and his date of birth, date of death, Hebrew star, Mogen David, the letters at the very bottom in Hebrew indicating the equivalent of a resting in peace, of being bound up with the rest of the souls for eternity. Then I chose to place on his gravestone something I felt was truly reflective of him, not only for me and the family but for all of the people who knew him. What I had chiseled on his stone was "The world is a profoundly emptier place without you."

However, it is one thing to do that on paper, it is quite another to actually see it in stone. I have seen my husband's name on all kinds of things – credits for music, for commercials, for promotions of educational facilities, you name it and his name is there. But to see his name on a gravestone, a man so young, was still jolting, even though I knew what it was and was prepared for it.

This had been a year for some rather horrific firsts, certainly for me personally. The loss of my husband and then the September 11th catastrophe that struck all of us, but oddly enough it also was a phenomenally unusual year in terms of weather. When I was in Ireland in October, the lowest tide ever recorded occurred, which I took as an omen because it was sort of a low ebb for me, too. When I was there in February and the wind was wailing and howling, they had the highest tides recorded in a hundred years. Then, the day we had the unveiling scheduled for my husband at the cemetery in Houston, it was the coldest day on record ever in Houston for that day. It was bitter, it was biting, it was windy, it was pretty reflective of how I think those of us there felt.

We opted to do a private family unveiling because, when I polled the family, the feeling was, and I totally agreed, that we had been through such a difficult year, and this was going to be such an emotional moment, we didn't need the pressure of outsiders. We really just needed to be with each other. After the unveiling, which is a very brief ceremony, we came back to my house for a brunch.

Fortunately, the weather lifted a little, the sun came out, and we were able to turn loose some of the bigger kids who could run off some of their pent-up energy. Instead of racing through the house, they were able to go outside, which was certainly a gift to the rest of us.

I am writing this particular part of my account on the 14th of March, which was always a very special day for me because it was the day I met my husband. It also, of course, is the same date I knew he was going to die. I began wearing his wedding ring around my neck on that day and have worn it ever since. I eventually decided to remove it and put it in the safe-deposit box once we had completed the entire commemorative year. I think it would be lovely for the son of his son to have this wedding ring when he himself gets married. It's probably important that I begin to think about moving myself in some ways forward in this area, although it is a very difficult and a painful thing to do.

We have yet to face the commemoration, the Yahrzeit of my husband's death. That will happen on the weekend following his actual death, on the weekend of the 22nd and 23rd of March. All of the family will be in town, which is very good. This will give us an opportunity to be at services together, to really put a ribbon around a full year of mourning, of grieving, of loss, of anger, of all of the things that go with the sudden and unexpected death of a person who was such a dynamic part of the lives of his family and everyone he touched.

As previously mentioned, the actual anniversary of my husband's death is the 20th of March. I am not sure who she knew or how she was able to do this, but my daughter's mother-in-law, who lives in New York, arranged for a commemorative Mass to be offered on the 20th of March for Larry at St. Patrick's Cathedral in New York City. He had a special affection for St. Pat's, and whenever we went to New York we would always pay a visit to the Cathedral and he would ask me to explain the various symbols and the Latin meanings. This is also a person who loved to see his name in lights and loved to hear his name announced in wonderful places like St. Patrick's Cathedral, so this would have been a most auspicious occasion for him.

I wanted to be there for this because in some special sense I would have felt his presence. Also, I wanted to be there for Marilyn, who had arranged this. It was a very gracious thing to do. It afforded me an opportunity to go up-state to visit my parents for a few days and then to come back to New York City and spend a couple of days there.

The day before the 20th was gorgeous, the day after was gorgeous, the 20th was horrific. It rained, it poured, it blew, it was cold. It was as if the heavens were weeping along with us. In addition to that, it was early morning and it was dark. So as we were making our way up Fifth Avenue at about 7:30, it seemed to be kind of an appropriate mood. Nature was providing the best kind of backdrop and atmosphere.

Before the service began, a woman stood and announced from the pulpit that this Mass was being offered in commemoration of Larry J. Sachnowitz, and I knew that wherever he was, he was loving it.

The reading was from the Book of Daniel, the story of Shadrach, Meshach and Abednego in the fiery furnace. They were amongst the exiles of Judah that King Nebuchadnezzar had brought into Babylon. They were ordered to worship the king and a false God. They refused and were thrown into the fiery furnace. After considerable time and considerable fuel, they were not consumed. The hairs on their bodies were not even singed. They were brought forth unharmed from the fiery furnace and, of course, this was a great testimony to the God of the Israelites.

I could not help but reflect, being that I am a Jewish woman who came from a Catholic background and now I'm in a Catholic Church for this mass for my Jewish husband, which is most weird, I could not help but reflect on whether or not God was suffering memory loss or whether God only dealt well with small numbers. Where was the God of the Israelites when the six million were being consumed by the fiery furnaces in Nazi Germany? Probably I was the only person in the place who was giving that kind of thought to the reading.

Following the service, we headed down to the World Trade Center, to ground zero. Marilyn had arranged for us to get tickets to the observation platform. It is an amazing place. It is so huge in comparison to what it looks like in pictures and on television. The enormity of it is horrific. You look at this hole in the ground that goes down several stories, this gaping wound in the earth that was left by the destruction of these buildings, and, if nothing else, it certainly steels the resolve of any American to do whatever is required to see that this never happens to us again.

It's a place where people come to observe and to pay tribute. They bring commemorative items, they sign their names on a board in ink that does not run when it rains. People bring flowers, and they just stand there and look and ponder. They're very respectful, and they wait in long lines, and they wait in all kinds of weather. It is truly, in many ways, the feeling one gets of being at a very holy shrine.

To be there on that day in my life, thinking of what this kind of loss means to so many other families, was a very moving and a very special moment. I also then managed to, rain or no rain, trot around

Manhattan because that was something we always loved to do. That evening, I went to a Broadway show, which probably to many seems like an odd thing to do. But my husband would have given his eye teeth to be in show business. He loved to go to Broadway shows. So we went to a show, and I was able to actually enjoy it. I was able to laugh, I was grateful for the company, and it was a moment to move me forward into the next phase of my life, my alone life.

The last event we actually had to get through as a family was the service at the synagogue observing the anniversary of his death. There are certain hymns and certain prayers that cause me to dissolve into tears and they certainly did that evening and probably will forever.

While my husband was alive he and another friend of his from San Antonio who in a name of a third friend, donated a set of the *Encyclopedia Judaic* to a Christian clergyman on an annual basis for his church. The decision was made to continue this and to add Larry's name. We had this special ecumenical moment going on at the time of his Yahrzeit and a small dinner for the recipient and our family in the boardroom at the synagogue following the service. This was a really loving thing for us to have this intimate moment with the rabbi, and his family, the reverend and his family and our family. It was a lovely fitting way to close the year.

Now, when I hear someone talk about "walking through the valley of the shadow of death," I realize that what I live with is the shadow. The horrible acute pain is no longer there, but the shadow of the loss colors everything and hovers over everything. Working through that will take a lot longer than a year. Somehow I had the feeling, and it was not an accurate feeling at all, that once the year was over I would be in a position to really feel a sense of completeness because I had devised rituals to commemorate events and commemorate experiences, yet that really is not true.

What has set in, and I wasn't prepared for it, is a deep loneliness. It isn't the looking at the door at 6:00 or 7:00 each evening and waiting for someone to come walking through. That has passed. It is the deep loneliness of being on your own for probably the rest of your life. It is the realization that when someone as integral to a family as a father and a husband dies, it isn't just the loss of that one person that happens, it is the change of the whole relationship of everyone.

It is like a mobile over a baby's crib. If you take one thing off, everything is sort of out of kilter. So when you take away a player as significant as Larry, everything now tilts into to different directions. People have to renavigate and renegotiate relationships in ways that they did not have to when he was here and we were a much more intact family.

All of that is a learning experience for everyone concerned. However, it is important, and, I think, perhaps an important lesson for women to come to understand that, when you have suffered this loss and you have worked through the loss and you have learned to become self-reliant and independent, there is a freedom that is empowering. It is the knowledge that, "I can do these things."

Did I want to do them? No. Would I like to go back to the old ways? Oh, yes! Am I able to do that? I am not. But I am able to take care of myself, I am able to make it alone, I am able to make good sound decisions that are for my own welfare and my own well-being. That is a very strengthening feeling. Once you get there, it gives you a kind of courage to go forward with your life.

I wish to leave that message with anyone who is walking the steps one needs to walk to get from loss, through grief, through anger, through depression to the small baby steps you begin to make when you come through the other end. When you kind of lift the veil and can see yourself as an autonomous person who needs to be able to look after herself, who will have friends and family and experiences that will be very different from before, but who is capable of doing what needs to be done and doing it with a certain pride and satisfaction.

That is a very enabling moment in allowing you to go forward into the rest of your life. My husband felt that life was to be lived, it was a banquet, and it was to be savored. The very last thing he would have ever wanted was for me to crawl into a shell and to give up on life and merely to exist for the remainder of my days. He would want me to live a life. He mentioned to me on the very last journey from Ireland as we were driving through the mountain pass that he loved and adored, saying in his very prescient way, "Suzanne, if anything happens to me, I want you to really consider building a life for yourself in Ireland. You could do that. You could create a new life for yourself here, and it would be good for you to do."

He was right. I am able to do that both in Houston and in Ireland. It is not an easy thing to do, but life is such a gift and life is so precious that to squander it by wallowing in self-pity or anger or any of the negative feelings that can accompany such an experience is to waste this most precious of gifts. It only comes around once and it's only for a very limited number of days.

The coins in your purse are not going to be replenished. Once you've spent the days of your life, the coin of the realm of your life, it's over, you don't get a second chance. The opportunity to appreciate and value life and living is much more poignant, much more tender than it was prior to having gone through this dreadful experience and this loss.

So to be able to live, not just exist, is one of the amazing gifts that comes from working through the experience of death. It's a life lesson that would have been much more readily received in some other fashion, but unfortunately that wasn't the way it was to happen. I lost my husband at a very young age, a man who should have lived to see his grandchildren grow and prosper and thrive, a man who should have lived to enjoy all of the things he worked a lifetime for. My husband was a man who should have gone into his old age enjoying and benefiting from the honors that come from those experiences.

That was not to be. Therefore, I live my life and in a sense the life that he was denied for the both of us. I hope it will be in an honorable and credible way so that wherever he is, he is looking and saying, "Well done, well done," and he would laugh at some of the things that have happened, and that is an essential part of going forward with living.

When you've cried all the tears you think you are capable of crying, it is time then to think about smiling again and to look at life with the eyes of someone who says, "Yes!" The great affirmative, "Yes, I will go on, I can go on, I was loved and I loved in return." That is the most strengthening experience and, because of that, I would not betray that love by negating the life that is left to me.

As Seamus Heaney, the Pulitzer Prize winning poet, says:

"Death doesn't banish someone out of your consciousness, but they're a part of the light in your head."

I dedicated this work to my husband, who I described as the light of my life. He will always be the light in my head, and I say to you my darling - *"lux perpetua."*

Heartbeats:

• Be sure your memories of the past do not obliterate your vision of the future.

• Say thank you a lot, it works miracles.

• Treasure the quirky as well as the familiar.

• Use your check list of warning signs to keep yourself okay; A.) Why am I still unable to get over this? B.) Do I sleep too little or too much? C.) The same with eating. D.) Do I drink too much? E.) Do I hide behind frenetic activity? If yes, get help, that's what it's there for.

• Children grieve differently and need reassurance over and over again in an age appropriate manor.

• Rabbi Greenberg, "To confront death without being overwhelmed, driven to evasions or dulling of the senses is to be given life again as a daily gift."

• To be able to live not just exist is one of the amazing gifts that comes from working through the experience of death.

• Say yes, the great affirmation to life, to your love and even to your loss.

• The acceptance of what you couldn't control will allow you to bring a finality to your tragedy.

• Life is too good, too wonderful, and too precious to waste.

An Album

Larry at two years of age.

Four-year-old Suzanne.

Larry, already entertaining at eleven.

Larry and Suzanne,
1981.

145

At home with the cows.

The house during construction phase.

Inside our home.

A view from the house.

Shoreline near our Irish residence.

Wildflower meadow of our Irish home.

Larry at Marfield House in Ireland

Bishop, the family dog.

Larry at Glendelough.

Family gathering for Suzanne's sixtieth birthday.

Our last photo together, February 2001.

David and Suzanne Syme and family.